THE LONG WAY HOME

Books in the Sequence *The Sensual World*
By the Same Author

THE GARDENS OF CAMELOT
THE ALTAR IN THE LOFT
THE DRUMS OF MORNING
THE GLITTERING PASTURES
THE NUMBERS CAME
THE LAST OF SPRING
THE PURPLE STREAK
THE WILD HILLS
THE HAPPY HIGHWAYS
THE SOUND OF REVELRY
THE MOON IN MY POCKET
THE LICENTIOUS SOLDIERY
THE BLOOD-RED ISLAND
THE GORGEOUS EAST
THE DOGS OF PEACE
THE LIFE FOR ME
THE VERDICT OF YOU ALL
THE TANGERINE HOUSE
THE QUEST FOR QUIXOTE
THE WINTRY SEA
THE GHOST OF JUNE
THE CAVES OF HERCULES
THE LONG WAY HOME

Supplementary
THE WORLD IS YOUNG
THE MAN IN EUROPE STREET
THE CIRCUS HAS NO HOME

THE LONG WAY HOME

Being the Penultimate Book in the Sequence
THE SENSUAL WORLD

Rupert Croft-Cooke

W. H. Allen
London
A division of Howard & Wyndham Ltd
1974

© Rupert Croft-Cooke 1974
This book or parts thereof may not be
reproduced in any form whatsoever
without permission in writing.

Printed and bound in Great Britain by
T. & A. Constable Ltd, Edinburgh
for the publishers, W. H. Allen & Co. Ltd,
44 Hill Street, London W1X 8LB.

ISBN 0 491 01502 X

Contents

			Page
Chapter One	Normandy	. . . . .	7
Chapter Two	Las Palmas	. . . . .	23
Chapter Three	Gibraltar	. . . . .	58
Chapter Four	Cyprus	. . . . .	74
Chapter Five	Tunis	. . . . .	101
Chapter Six	Dublin	. . . . .	137
Chapter Seven	Ceuta and Melilla	. . . .	174
Chapter Eight	Cologne	. . . . .	188

To
Joan
Notwithstanding

One

Normandy

On the day on which I was to leave Tangier after fourteen years of living there I was roused early because I had to go down to the docks before eight o'clock, the hour at which the small French steamer sailed. Anna McKew, my hostess during the days since I had left my flat in the town, drove me down in the stifling heat of an August morning and came on board with me. She waved before getting into her car and driving away, and she left me to a kind of loneliness and uncertainty such as I had not felt for many years.

During the period I had lived in Tangier I had left it many times, of course—for England, France, Spain, India and Czecho-Slovakia, but never without the intention to return, never without a home there which would be waiting for me when the journey was over. Now the flat I had occupied was empty and my possessions were in store waiting to be shipped to wherever I should find a home. Joseph, my Indian secretary, so much more a permanence in my life than any home since he had started working for

7

me twenty-five years earlier, had left for a holiday in India and I thought that almost every one of those I had seen often of recent years was lying asleep in the villas of the town that overlooked the docks or was starting another of the pleasant Moroccan days I was deliberately leaving.

Why? I remember asking myself that for the hundredth time that morning as I looked back on the white Moorish buildings which crowded one another up the slopes to the Kasbah, the familiar vista of the town I had so often seen from approaching ships. Why had I quite suddenly decided to cut loose and quit the home I had made and the sunlit life I had enjoyed for so long? Partly no doubt it was the degeneration and change in Tangier which I have already described in *The Caves of Hercules*. Partly it was a foreboding about the future of Morocco itself, which seemed to promise chaos and old night in the not too distant future and had already inspired whispers of the Morocconization which would one day cause all foreign property in the country to be threatened with seizure. Partly, again, it was because I did not wish to end my days in this country, so unremittingly alien to me even after I had lived in it so long. Partly because I wanted to see it in perspective and from afar, in order to write a novel about it. But most of all, I realized, because I was a natural nomad and had already broken my vows by staying too long here, a nomad not only by habit but by heredity and upbringing. This may seem a bold claim for the son of a Surrey stockbroker who only once left England, and that for a brief holiday, but I could recognize in my father all the symptoms of the bedouin, however tidy and conventional his commuting life. Though—as I have recounted in earlier books in this series—he lived his whole life in the Home Counties, he had changed homes every few years from his marriage in 1896 to his death in 1935, occupying fourteen houses, each of which he intended to inhabit till he died, and in each of which he made a garden. Inheriting the habits of my greatly-loved father I had myself occupied a dozen homes before I came to Tangier, and had many times congratulated myself on having settled there at last, and believed that I should remain there. But nomadism is not just a pedantic word for a restless disposition, it is a way of life that springs up in some individuals, perhaps from their earliest forefathers, and this it had done in me, driving me away from habits and surroundings, from friends and comforts, to find a new way of life, a new place in which to settle, and totally new experiences. Many of these might not give me the contentment which Tangier had given me, but I had to discover that.

> *Come, my friends, 'Tis not too late to seek a newer world.*
> *. . . My purpose holds*
> *To sail beyond the sunset, and the baths*
> *Of all the western stars, until I die.*
> *Tho' much is taken, much abides; and tho'*
> *We are not now that strength which in old days*
> *Moved earth and heaven; that which we are, we are;*
> *Made weak by time and fate, but strong in will*
> *To strive, to seek, to find, and not to yield.*

Good old Tennyson! He always had a line to match one's aspirations however banal, so that he added a touch of Victorian-Heroic even to one's most prosaic and twentieth century thoughts.

To quote his *Ulysses* in illustration of what might be considered no more than the departure of a not very successful writer from one Mediterranean resort of income tax-dodgers to look for another will seem pretentious perhaps, but I did not think it so as I watched the outline of

Tangier grow hazy and disappear from sight. It seemed justified to me who had learned to live twice, once in actuality, episode by episode and scene by scene, and once in recollection as I write these books.

Fourteen years, after all, is a large part of one man's life. I had come to the city fresh—or not so fresh—from the loathsome events which had befallen me in 1953 and been healed and purified by the sunlight and love I had found there. I had written fourteen books, enjoyed sex in delirious variety, learned to make a semi-tropical garden and to cook; I had travelled and become acquainted with an immense number of people whom I found intensely interesting; I had talked whole nights away and consciously watched the changes in the world during all those fourteen years, and *could* say that though much was taken, much abided. Perhaps at this setting forth I had not quite the old eagerness, or was it impatience? But I still had health and curiosity enough to look forward to the unknown pleasures and experiences of the future.

2

It was a French packet boat on which I had embarked, running regularly from Casablanca to Marseilles and calling every few trips at Tangier. The accommodation was spartan and the food no more than sufficient, for this French Line had been formed to meet the needs of the *colons* and soldiers when Morocco had been a French possession.

In the bar that evening I met an elderly Frenchman, one of the few who had held on to their agricultural lands and seemed to regret having done so. He was obsessed with worries about the future of the world and believed that Armageddon was close upon us.

'Close?' he said when I showed myself less given to such biblical fancies. 'It is upon us now. You saw what happened in the Six-Day War last year? It was only the beginning. Have you not read the Book of Revelation in the Bible? You shouldn't laugh that off, you know. We are told that the last great war between the nations will be there, in Palestine. Perhaps you think it's a coincidence? Read it! The very atom bomb is predicted there.'

'Do you think we shall live to see it?' I asked curiously, for he was in his seventies.

'Perhaps not. But it will come. Armageddon. The end of the world. The Jews have always been the most fateful race in the world and now that they occupy their own promised land we shall see . . .'

I forget what we should see according to the old French colonial. Apocalyptic things, I seem to remember, which showed the hostilities between the Arabs and Israel in the previous year to have been a prologue to the war of all nations. I have small patience with this kind of conclusion-drawing from old prophecies which is so tempting to the superstitious, almost as tempting as the suppressed theory of a Russian professor that the destruction of Sodom and Gomorrah had been brought about by an atomic attack from people from another planet so beautiful that they were mistaken for angels from God, almost as tempting as the 'certain knowledge' of some people that every meteorite or speck in the sky is a 'flying object' from outer space. For those who take pleasure in such winsome superstitions the past is as good a hunting-ground for delusions as the present or for that matter the future. So I listened respectfully to the old Frenchman's prognostic and invited him to have a drink which he enjoyed so smilingly that the approach of Armageddon seemed to be forgotten.

Meanwhile we were ploughing our way north to Marseilles, a city I had known well, but of which except in fiction I had written little. I recalled it briefly in *The Ghost of June*: 'I came to that city, then so mysterious, so luridly Mediterranean, so little changed in essence since Dumas pictured it, just before the war and like any other inquisitive tourist made for the Vieux Port and spent several days and nights in its narrow alleys. I had no need of a camera for what I saw and learned then remained vividly in my mind and brought me the only sizeable sum of money I have ever made by writing. For when I heard how the Germans had razed the whole *quartier* with all its rat-runs and escape routes and vice and crime after giving the inhabitants three hours to leave it, I went back after the war and found a heap of rubble and sand-dunes in its place, and determined to write a book about those last three hours and some of the people trapped there. The money did not come from the book, needless to say, but from the film *Seven Thunders* that was made from it.'

This gave little reality to the city as I first knew it in 1938. I had weakly undertaken then to use my car for a holiday with a man named Curtis Brown, a literary agent who acted for me, but during the long drive southward I had grown bored and insisted on giving a lift to two students who were trying to get to the South of France by *auto-stop*. One of them was the younger son of a man named Léon Sée, a journalist and the manager of the giant boxer Primo Carnera. Dropping the literary agent at St Remy, I drove the two young men to Marseilles and remember that on our first evening there we did the two things most expected of visitors—ate *bouillabaisse* in a fisherman's restaurant in the Old Port, and amused ourselves as *voyeurs* in an over-furnished brothel where we watched a middle-aged shop-

keeper who wore woollen combinations and a bowler hat
and tenaciously kept both on until the paunchy whore he
had chosen had earned her money.

This was the first of several nights spent in the lurid
region of the Vieux Port and days wandering up the Rue
Cannebière. It was from the recollections unconsciously
stored then in my mind that I was able to use Marseilles as a
background for my novel *Seven Thunders*. But there was
another visit soon after the war, and although I calculated
that it was less than ten years later than the first, it made
Marseilles seem to belong to another existence. I was
commissioned by an English illustrated magazine to write
an article about the city and was provided with an introduction to the Chief of Police who in turn provided me with a
couple of *flics* to show me round.

But the whole region of the Vieux Port had by then been
blotted out and left a sandy and stony hillside completely
bare where the maze of streets with its *bistros* and bars, its
estaminets and *dancings*, had crowded one another in noisy
competition for the custom of tourists, and where a Senegal-
ese giant had stood, seemingly immovable at the door of a
brothel, splendid in gold braid. The Protestant Mission
with textural posters which had once competed with the
neon bar signs had been as it were blown away with the
rest of the buildings. Later that hillside was to be covered
with concrete structures, offices, shops, blocks of flats, but
as I saw it in 1948 re-building had not commenced and the
bare slopes were as the Germans had left them. This gave
me a quotation from Ovid with which to open my novel
Seven Thunders: Iam seges est ubi Troia fuit, 'now there are
cornfields where once Troy stood'.

A few years later I returned to foregather with a young
French friend whom I had first met in Pau (another scene

for a novel of mine—*Brass Farthing*). Gui Turban lived in the suburb of Mazargues, almost in the shadow of that huge housing unit planned by Le Corbusier as a self-contained community, so that I have become familiar with two of that remarkable architect's creations, this one on the outskirts of Marseilles and Barcelona's more eccentric apartment block.

Yet now that I was actually approaching Marseilles from the sea, it was not, for some undiscoverable reason, the old city crawling with vice and lice which I had found before the war, or the huge metropolis which had risen in its place since then, but one which I had only pictured in boyish daydreams inspired by Alexandre Dumas the elder. One of the few books which served as furniture in the philistine homes of my dear parents had been *The Count of Monte Cristo* in a clear-type edition. The volume had been purchased with a small collection of books from the previous tenants of our house in Chipstead when we had moved there in 1908, a collection which included I remember some novels by Rhoda Broughton and one by Robert Hichens called *Barbary Sheep* which was confiscated from me by my mother as undesirable reading. *The Count of Monte Cristo* counted as a 'classic' and was therefore permitted and I devoured it, hungry for something more highly-coloured than *The Spy at Sedgemere School* and *The Mystery at Melford Manor*, current serials in *Chums*.

I identified myself wholly with Dantes whom I first met in a heavily painted dockland scene and followed with gusto through his escape from the Château d'If and his fabulous enrichment and revenges. I remember lying in the Surrey orchard reading that story when I was six or seven years old, but did not recall the scenes which Dumas or his illustrator made so vivid until I found them again in

Joseph Conrad's *Suspense* ten years later. Why all this literary image, so long forgotten or buried under the realities I had discovered in later years, should have returned to me on this occasion I cannot decide. I am not being affected or theatrical, or claiming that I expected to see the people of Napoleonic Marseilles in the streets of the city that August morning, but it is a fact that as the little steamer approached Marseilles, the scenes I had dreamed up as a boy were more vivid in prospect than the great new buildings that I knew I should find.

As I did, with an altogether new brashness and modernity. The only taxi I found outside the Customs Sheds charged double the fare to take me to the railway station unless I was willing to wait for an unspecified period to share it with someone else who might need a taxi going that way, and since I had to catch the Paris train I was forced to agree to this blackmailing trick which I found was common in provincial France at that time. I remember being rushed through the crowded streets, unable to glimpse more than a kaleidoscopic swirl of shop fronts.

But once in one of the swift and comfortable trains that linked Marseilles with Paris I decided to enjoy the *table d'hôte* lunch, such as only in France is provided for railway passengers. When I saw that each menu was signed by the chef I felt that I was truly back in the country—not that of Dumas or of pre-war excellence, but France all the same, France which I had so often maintained was the most civilized country in the modern world.

3

Robert Cahiza, the French friend of my boyhood, was waiting for me at the station in Paris and I went at once to his home to discuss my movements for the future. I told him that I proposed to find a home in Dieppe on the coast of Normandy. This was my first scheme, in fact, for the life I wanted to make.

In theory it seemed not such a bad idea as I enumerated the advantages. Television, which had begun to become important to me during my last visits to England, could be watched from the French coast I had been told. The climate could be no worse than that of Kent less than thirty miles away. In a couple of hours or so I could reach London at any time and so attend to those aspects of my work which necessitated my 'keeping in touch'. I spoke the language, was at home with the people and of course enjoyed French food and wine. There would not be the persistent sunshine of North Africa but I did not believe I had become so dependent on the heat of the sun that I could not go back to the climate euphemistically called temperate which I had known in childhood and young manhood.

Besides, the port of Dieppe was associated in my long and indefatigable memory with many pleasant occasions, from my first leaving England at the age of nineteen to spend a summer in France as tutor to young Fredrik Wachtmeister, as I have recorded in *The Glittering Pastures*, to many later crossings from Newhaven which by chance had always been smooth occasions. It was on the night of May 19 1897 that Oscar Wilde having left prison that morning, crossed the Channel with More Adey and was met at Dieppe by Ross and Reggie Turner to breakfast in the Hotel Sandwich, before going farther up the coast to the village of Berneval. All through the remainder of that summer Oscar lived in the neighbourhood, visiting Dieppe with Ernest Dowson and being visited there by Charles Conder, Dal Young, William Rothenstein, André Gide and other friends. He was quite happy in the little seaside town and the neighbouring village of Berneval and his letters during that summer are full of spirit and gaiety, and only after he had spent a day in Rouen with Bosie and the winter was approaching, did he discover that he must leave it, and wrote to Ross: 'I simply cannot stand Berneval. I nearly committed suicide there last Thursday—I was so bored.'

I do not know quite why I chose Dieppe from among all the coastal towns of Normandy and Brittany, with several of which I was more familiar. Not, I think the Wilde association, and certainly not the memory of the disastrous Dieppe Raid which took place while I was in Madagascar, or the annual raids of English tourists who came ashore in as many thousands during the summer. I decided on it rather casually as a likely place and took the train to it without having made any preparations, delighted at the sense of personal freedom which this pin-stick of a choice gave me.

A chatty taximan at the station took me to a hotel which he recommended. 'It is not,' he said, 'one of the big luxury hotels on the sea-front. They charge thousands of francs for a peep at the sea, down there. You will find many *plats* in their *tables d'hôte*. Many. But you won't eat so well as in the place I will show you. It is not an *hotel de grand luxe*, you understand, but it is *assez confortable* and not excessively expensive.'

When we reached it, a good solid building at a street corner overlooking nothing more festive or seaside than a busy crossroads, he jumped out and entered the hotel ahead of me doubtless to arrange his commission. When I was younger this would have roused all kinds of suspicions in me and put me on my guard against the 'continental trickery' which we English once suspected everywhere abroad but with more experience I recognized it as correct and everyday procedure which would cost me nothing.

In that I was right. I was shown a large Victorian bedroom with a nineteenth-century bathroom attached and went down to a rather splendid dining-room for lunch. Was not *à la Dieppoise* a standard term in French cookery? 'A method of preparation' says Larousse, 'special to sea-water fish. Fish *à la Dieppoise* is cooked in white wine, garnished with mussels and shelled fresh-water crayfish tails, and masked with a white wine sauce made with the cooking stock of the fish and mussels.' As I finished a sole prepared in this way with which I had enjoyed a bottle of Muscadet, dry as a bone and well chilled, Tangier seemed a long way in the past and I saw myself remaining in this friendly little town for years.

4

It was not to be. Finding homes comes as second nature to me as I was to find confirmed in the years ahead, but it cannot be quite as easy as that. I could not leave Tangier after fourteen years and within a week settle in a suitable permanent home in Normandy. I tried. I began on the following day the weary pursuit, familiar to all home-seekers, from the offices of one estate agent to another, through the advertisements, the enquiries among chance acquaintances and the rest which may lead to success.

I had not yet come to realize that what had changed about house property in France, as in England and the rest of Europe and indeed throughout most of the world, was that unfurnished flats or houses were no longer rentable. They could occasionally be purchased, with or without a mort-gage, or they could be rented if they were 'furnished', because putting into them a few pieces of bric-a-brac enabled the owners to eject their tenants at brief notice, but the practice common throughout my life and my father's life, of renting living accommodation on a lease binding to both tenant and owner, no longer existed. In Tangier it had been easy to find a flat or a villa at little more than £3 a week and I had innocently supposed that in France, though it would be more expensive, I would find modest unfurnished accomodation by that mixture of instinct and good luck which had served me so well in these matters all my life.

I climbed an ugly hill on the landward side of the town to find one of those streets of identical terrace houses of red brick such as I had so often motored through on the way to the town centre in northern industrial France, streets like our own in mining and manufacturing districts which were (fortunately perhaps) erased by the blitz. A stuffy interior of two rooms with ugly but inadequate furniture, an outlook on a similar small house across the road, with a mile's walk uphill from the shops and seashore could be mine for twenty pounds a week during the winter months. A single room for sale over a shop in the centre of Dieppe, with a rusty bathroom and an ancient geyser and a six-foot square kitchen was proudly offered to me by one agent for £8000 if I did not mind the suicidal dark staircase and the din of traffic below. A great opportunity occurred to rent furnished a comfortable family flat overlooking the sea since its owner had been moved to Paris and wished to keep it for his retirement in a few years' time. This sounded promising enough but when I examined it and found it so over-bearingly furnished with vast quantities of ornaments, the elaborate patterns of curtains and carpets which spread like a nightmare about me, feather beds and such an air of having been occupied for years by a numerous family whose sense of hygiene had been perceptibly lacking, when I was shown the primitive furnace in a cellar by which alone the place could be heated and learned that the rent was £30 a week— about my total earnings—my interest and indeed my hopes began to flag. Another agent took me by car twelve miles out of the town to where a hideous nineteenth-century *château* was being converted into flats, most of which had already been bought by young couples with children, and explained that I could purchase a cubby-hole on the third floor for £10,000 though I would, the agent frankly pointed out, need a car since no buses passed near the building.

I did not give up. I had been told that though in Dieppe it was difficult to find any kind of home, in other towns on the coast of Normandy, and Brittany from Calais to Cherbourg it was quite impossible so I went down to the dockland slums where a rather shifty old gentleman had bought up most of the property and would have a shop with living accommodation over it for sale in some months' time. This might have provided a picturesque kind of life for a young artist surrounded by his own colony, but I could not see it as a quiet dwelling-place for me and Joseph.

Then as I was returning in heavy rain to the door of the hotel which was at the head of some worn and slippery steps, I slid and fell full length and for some minutes was unable to get up. I shouted to several pedestrians for help but watched them hurry past on the other side, doubtless thinking I was an English drunk. After a while I struggled to my feet and managed to get to the hotel lounge where I promptly fainted.

Shaken by this mishap and temporarily lamed I decided to leave for London and did so, with my first attempt to find a home behind me.

It was not merely Dieppe which seemed to me at that time to have failed my expectations, but all France. Paris I knew to be out of the question because of the vast expense of living there and the impossibility of movement in the city, but I had thought that one of the less notable seaside towns, over-crowded in the summer but pleasant for the rest of the year, might provide a refuge from which I could visit London when I wanted. I remembered the smiling welcome of the French whenever I had crossed the Channel before the war, not only of the shopkeepers and *hoteliers* and *restaurateurs* but of people casually met everywhere. They seemed to like the English spending holidays, then so inexpensively, among them, and from the summer of 1922 when the Wachtmeisters had taken me to Paris, Le Touquet and Aix-les-Bains, to the winter of 1938 which I had spent in Alsace with Robert Cahiza, I had loved every visit to France. Even since the war when I had spent long periods in Paris, in the Landes, in Pau and up and down the country on my way to and from Tangier, I had persuaded myself that France was still welcoming and cheerful. But I detected, or believed I detected in that month of August 1968 a new sullenness among the people and knew that though I should always respect their unique qualities I did not want to live among them.

Doubtless it was too broad a conclusion to draw from this brief stay but the conviction must have been growing in me for years and now overwhelmed me that the Englishman's old dream of La Belle France, the paradise just across the Channel, the place of entrancing naughtiness where the pound sterling could purchase unlimited salaams and smiles from the amiable peasantry, the gourmet's paradise where Lucullan delicacies were bought with the loose change in one's pocket and where a *château* beside a river as a home was within any Englishman's means; where policemen were comedians' stock-in-trade and casinos in palmy resorts gathered the illustrious from all the civilized world to enjoy unheard of extravagance and watch fortunes made and lost on the roulette wheel; where kings and queens from all the courts in Europe came to relax and have hotels named after them and where *patisseries*, *perfumes*, *bibelots*, *aperitifs*, *demi-mondaines* and *tapettes* were obtainable in bewildering varieties, and finally where the greatest wines were supplied almost free to one patronising any restaurant.

I was old enough to have known this France, or one very like it and to have seen the fabulous *Côte d'Azur* in its prime. But there was no point in trying to recall it and although I have continued to enjoy the amenities of France in the six years since that August I have never considered it again as a possible place of residence.

Two

Las Palmas

I did not spend long in England at that time because I was still apprehensive about the Income Tax Inspector, not having yet fully realized that my paltry earnings from the books I had to turn out at regular intervals were not sufficient to bring me into his net. I had always resented being called a tax-dodger, pointing out hopefully, and as it later transpired quite truthfully, that my income did not make tax-dodging worth while. But I feared the forms, the interviews, the discussions with accountants and the polite menaces of the tax-collector and believed that if I stayed longer than three months in the country I should be responsible to him. It was not for another six years, and seven moves later, that I realized the truth, that my earnings, those of a reasonably successful full-time professional writer, amounted to rather less than those of unskilled or lower-paid manual workers and so were taxed on the same level as these, unless in some particular year there fell to me one of the chancy rewards of my job, the sale of film rights or a glint of momentary best-sellerdom. So long as I remained no more successful than all but the half dozen truly prosperous writers in the country, I could afford to live, penuriously but without the frequent need to seek Public Assistance, in provincial England. But I had not yet awakened to this, so that in the chilly autumn of 1968 the bogey of taxation kept me abroad.

I remained in London for a month, staying as usual with Patrick Kinross in Little Venice, then went to the home of my friend Joan Cave who with her scientist husband lived in a great Victorian family house on the outskirts of Pembury. I was thus in my own country, if any could be said to be that, a few miles from Tonbridge School and Cage House, from Ticehurst and Tunbridge Wells, from Wrotham and Longfield, from all the places which had been familiar to me since boyhood. There, with cosy family conversation round log-fires at night and in the daytime searches for early English watercolours in the neighbouring shops, and hours of work on *Exiles* the novel I should publish in the following year, I faced my first spell of English hard weather since I had left for Tangier in 1954.

Little wonder that I began to long for the sunshine I had enjoyed so long and, as I cannot avoid doing, began to search for it in the past. In a life so dedicated to reminiscences and memories I became like a man searching through old scented trunks and boxes in the attic of his brain, looking for something which would brighten the present. I found it in Las Palmas, the capital of the Canary Islands.

The pictures that this old city raised in my recollection were vivid and happy and although reason told me curtly that I should not find much evidence of the place I had known, something must surely remain. I had come ashore on the most memorable voyage of my life—perhaps because it was the first—my journey at eighteen years old to Buenos Aires on a Lamport and Holt cargo boat out of Liverpool. I remember walking through narrow sunlit streets and buying cigarettes loose in a large box and a carved bone cigarette-holder which an Indian shopkeeper assured me was ivory. Two years later on my way home from Argentina I came ashore again in Las Palmas this time at night, and described the occasion in *The World is Young*: 'So we came to the Canary Isles, and saw the moon rise over Africa. I had long been congratulating myself on the fact that the next time I set foot on land it would be on the shores of the Fortunate Isles. Even as a child I had longed to see them, picturing them vaguely as a paradise of fruits and flowers and sunshine, where the staple industry was the snaring of canary birds for the maiden ladies and station-masters of the hyperborean realm of Britain. It was ten o'clock at night when the anchor cable at last paid out, in the roads off Las Palmas; and although the eight-hour fetish would be little regarded on these shores, it was reasonable to conclude that the work of the fowler would have ended for the day. But the lights of the town, twinkling across the dark water were irresistible, and, with a little suasion, we got leave to go ashore in the company's launch, which had brought the busy agent aboard. The boatmen, we were told, would wait for us till midnight at a convenient quay. Once aboard the lugger, however, the men informed us that, for a small consideration, they would await our return until any hour of the morning.

We landed in the purple African night, near a gravelled plaza. It took a little time to adjust my mind to the fact that the night *was* African, not South American. Cape Juby, on the mainland, was not much more than a hundred-and-twenty miles away, while thousands of miles separated us from the American continent; but the palm trees, the stucco houses, and general atmosphere of the place, made it seem little different from some seaboard town of Brazil. I was taken to a club near the harbour by a chance acquaintance. The gambling here seemed more solemn than in Brazil, but its results were no happier, and I was not sorry when it was indicated that the session was ended. It must have been well into the small hours when I went from the club into a cabaret near by. Splendid, indefatigable Canarios! London had been sent to bed these two or three hours past, but the light-hearted islanders were dancing still. When I entered the cabaret there were only two or three couples, it is true, in the dance hall—a large, airy room, with whitewashed walls picked out with sea-green stencillings. At first I feared I had arrived too late, but it appeared presently that I was a little too early. Whether it is the practice of the Canarios to go to bed at sunrise, or to get up early and bring the day in with dancing, is a matter about which I am still in doubt. However that may be, by three o'clock in the morning a dozen or more couples were on the floor, and more were drifting in. Towards sunrise it occurred to me that I had been fasting longer than an Englishman should; so I adjourned to the dining-room for a late supper or early breakfast of mixed grill and red Canary wine—all of it excellent in quality, and the whole bill amounting to less than a London waiter's tip. When I returned to the dance hall the company was gathered about the piano, and a young Canario with a mellifluous voice was singing Spanish songs. Our journey back to the ship was made in broad daylight.

But that was not all. I went out to South America again in 1936 on a ship of the Blue Star Line which again called at Las Palmas less than two months after the Spanish Civil War had begun, but found it as peaceful as in 1924. A young taxi-driver took me up to the hills and we sat together over the city we had left while he confided in me, as young Spaniards like to confide spontaneously in strangers, all about his life and what he thought of the war.

'I care nothing for governments,' he said. 'The Republic or the Falange are all one to me. All I want is to drive my taxi and earn a living. But I'm going to be called up at any moment and sent across to Spain to shoot other Spaniards. Why? Because I am already trained and twenty-two years old—just what they want as fodder. Who has a right to take a man's life from him? Franco? Azana? I want to live and let others live. But I shall be given a gun and told to shoot the enemy. Whose enemy? Not mine. I have no enemies. That's what war means.'

As though he had been inhospitable in telling me his troubles he became suddenly gay and friendly. We drove to a vantage point from which we could see the city and the infinite placid Atlantic below. We sat on the fresh grass with our backs to some rocks and a sudden comradeship grew between us, because I had some understanding of his predicament and he maintained an uninvidious attitude to a foreigner whose good fortune in not being due for conscription, or poor, or sex-starved, he remarked on with a sigh. But he returned to his complaint.

'Be damned to them!' he said. 'All the generals and politicians, the lot of them. They have their reasons for falling out. What reason have I? Yes, I'm a Spaniard and a Christian. I'm not *afraid* to fight, but it is against my will. This war should be fought by volunteers. There would be plenty of those to kill one another for what they believe in—the Falange, the CNT, what you like. If they want a war let them fight it and not force me and the other young men to take part. No one speaks for us—the uncommitted Spaniards. Do you realize, señor, that wherever you happen to be in Spain you find yourself in one camp or another? You'll be enlisted and trained and you'll fight. If this island had chanced to be held by the Government I should be fighting on the other side. What's the sense of it? How many people are *really* involved in this war, heart and soul? How many would really care who wins if they hadn't been dragged in? A few Anarchists. A few Syndicalists. A few CEDA men and Fascists. A few army officers who want promotion. But I speak for the youth of Spain, and we want none of it.'

I have, of course, paraphrased and made more articulate the words he used, but I have not distorted them. I made notes of his outbursts that night on board and though these are long since lost I have not forgotten the exact sense of them.

His name, ironically, was Jesús, and he took me later to a café to which the taxi-drivers went, so that when I returned through Las Palmas three months later I could enquire for him. He had been called up and killed on the Madrid front.

In all four of these brief visits I found Las Palmas a sweet and memorable city, a little down-at-heels as Spanish colonial towns usually were, but rich with luxuriant vegetation, smiling people and rococo architecture. It was now, I was told in 1968, still a free port, inexpensive and hospitable. I was warned that it was given over to tourism but in Tangier I had seen how little this damaged the residential part of the town and had faith in the essential *españolismo* of Las Palmas to make it habitable in spite of the alien holiday-makers.

It seemed in prospect a place in which to live and work and find contentment, and I decided to make the attempt.

2

For practical as well as sentimental reasons (having a good deal of luggage) I decided to approach Las Palmas as I had done in earlier years by ship. I was lucky to obtain, through an enterprising travel agent who usually specialized in instant air travel for pressmen and television reporters, a passage on one of the great liners which called in at the Canary Islands on her way to Cape Town. It was December and the ship was crowded with plutocratic winter holiday-makers bound for the sun, but there had been a last-minute cancellation which provided me with a cabin on A deck.

I gazed around me in the bar that evening before dinner noting my fellow-passengers so evidently prosperous and sleek and was thankful that I had only three days to spend among them—not time for those bright and commonplace conversations by which travelling Englishmen show themselves amicably disposed towards their fellows without ever revealing for a moment anything remotely personal or interesting. I exchanged banalities with a young Jewish businessman who explained to me how he had obtained one of the more expensive cabins and enquired about my own. When his wife joined him I saw that she was more experienced than he was in separating the sheep from the goats on the first evening aboard, that vital hour when associations may be formed which prove inescapable for the rest of the voyage. She quickly elicited from me the fact that I was travelling only as far as Las Palmas and led her husband away to seek more propitious acquaintances.

But I was mistaken if I supposed that the passengers were universally dull for on the following morning I met two men who would have stood out as unusual and likeable in any company. One was Lord Fraser of Lonsdale whom I saw moving freely through the smoke-room. I enjoyed a long conversation with him before realizing that he was totally blind. He had been, in fact, the Chairman of the Council of St Dunstan's since 1921 having lost his sight in the First World War. It would have been impudent on such small acquaintance to marvel at a man for his achievement and courage in having mastered one of the greatest disabilities of mankind (in his case inflicted in his twenty-first year), but I cannot refrain now from expressing the admiration I felt, imagining all that had gone to make from the shattered and sightless young soldier of 1917 this humorous imperturbable man who discussed such wide-ranging subjects with acumen and gusto. The pastime that pleased him most was the game of Bridge which he played with specially manufactured cards but unhesitatingly and, I was told, exceedingly well. He knew Stanley Shelbourne Taylor, my Uncle Toby, and my friend Jack Gerber, Anna McKew's father, another remarkable man, so that I may have appeared to him as one given to the hero-worship of unusual people.

My other meeting during those few days running southward was with a Canadian Professor of Philosophy whose name I have unfortunately forgotten as I have forgotten not one single name of the passengers on the *Holbein* in 1923. This was a man of great charm and modesty who startled me by actually respecting writers of fiction from his own heights of academic distinction. 'But you create,' he said. 'We only reason.' Encouraging words to me who needed encouragement from dons and other scholars, particularly as they seem in recent years, to have taken over all the prerogatives of the critic, infesting the offices of *The Times Literary Supplement*, once the home of the best literary criticism in England with their exhibitionistic beards and niggling opinions. My Canadian friend, although his work had been accorded a laudatory article in that weekly paper, regretted this tendency towards pedagogic infantilism as much as I did and tickled my ego by telling me so. The steward in charge of the ship's library had called his attention to me and my books, copies of which seemed to crop up then as now wherever books are lent, and so rarely in places where they are sold.

3

I went ashore in Las Palmas on a warm and sunny December morning and if I had hoped against all advice to find something left of the lazy old port with its cobbled streets and sleazy cafés and indolent people I was soon disillusioned. It was outwardly a brisk crowded city with tall blocks of offices and flats overhanging its shopping-streets, where articles found in all free ports were sold; cigars, fountain pens, electrical appliances and watches, all of dubious utility. The traffic fought its way through, scattering its oppressed pedestrians and there was not a donkey or a horse to be seen.

I made my way to the hotel in which I had reserved a room, only to be told that I could not keep it for more than nine days, before the Christmas holiday rush, for which all rooms had been reserved by Scandinavian holiday-makers, but as the hotel was expensive and its employees behaved with a patronising superiority which was new to me for all my forty years' familiarity with Spain, I was glad to know that I should have to find new quarters. There were, I was told, many furnished flats in the town and although they were rarely unoccupied for long I might be able to find one.

I did. It appeared that the vast hordes of holiday-makers who come to the Canary Islands chiefly from northern

Europe did not go to hotels which were expensive and—
even the best of them—dishonest, but crowded into sparsely
furnished flats, a large family to a room, in which they could
prepare the tinned food, manufactured cakes, sardines and
cereal products coloured to resemble pork, on which they
chiefly subsisted. In these flats they could use their transistor
radios as late and loudly as they pleased since all the other
inhabitants were of like mind and had the conventional idea
of a holiday, noise, scorched skins gained with the torture of
beach sunlight, unlimited liquor, and facilities for adultery
and mixed bathing. The whole town was full of such
apartments, offering two or three beds and children's cots
to each room, breakfasts consisting of luke-warm coffee and
dry sweet *bollos* or Spanish breakfast buns, so much inferior
to French *croissants*, hurried attentions from a couple of
cleaning women to each dozen or more flats, all for about
£20 per week, per person.

Every one of the older buildings had been divided up
into these nominally furnished apartments and more blocks
of them were rising all the time. It seemed that the Canarios,
whom I remembered as carefree and comatose loungers,
had managed to build or somehow obtain possession of
enough of these flats to keep themselves prosperous, and
the supply of Scandinavian and German workers, arriving
by every plane for their holiday was inexhaustible. The more
highly paid workers among the Swedes and Danes found
flats from which a glimpse of the sea could be caught, for
this was a status symbol and decided prestige amongst them
all. However crowded the beaches were, however shrill with
the yells of children or heavy with the stink of fried fish,
those resolutely stolid holiday-makers meant to remain
within walking-distance from the beach where they
reddened themselves in the blistering sunlight. So it was

that my plans for the next few weeks were forced on me. I found a 'service flat' in one of the less offensively over-crowded buildings, and moved into it from the hotel.

But I soon realized an even more discouraging fact about Las Palmas. I had arrived in December, but only minimally did the weather vary from the warmest months, remaining hot, damp, muggy all the year round except for an occasional brief and violent rain storm which came almost as a relief to the islanders. There were no seasons, no enlivening spring, no crisp and frosty weather, but always a monotonously placid climate with nothing to distinguish one time of year from another. I found this stifling, and when I was assured that so long as I remained in the Fortunate Isles I should find no variation in the conditions about me I began my first real doubts about the place.

There would also be no variation from the norm of the population, or at least from the population seen in the streets. They would be honest, hard-working, hard-drinking beefy blond proletarians from Scandinavia and Germany, lying on their bellies on the beach or shouting choruses in the bars. The Canarios were content to profit from them and remained indoors at night, while the shops and cafés catered for tourists almost exclusively. The whole town seemed in fact to be given over to them in appearance and spirit, and this was not just for a few weeks of holiday time but throughout the year. Like the weather they knew no variation but arrived by plane every week-end, stayed their fortnight, and were replaced by more from the same wintry sources of supply. Their employers were bound by Swedish law to give them not only the time for holidays with pay but also the arrangements for the holidays them-selves, and they could do this more cheaply in the Canaries than in Sweden, even allowing for the cost of air passages.

B

I had nothing against Scandinavians and certainly nothing against factory workers but to find this once flowery and indolent island possessed entirely by them, with their peeling skins and rowdy good-fellowship, was daunting to say the least of it.

But however critical I may sound in describing Las Palmas today, I was determined to enjoy it. A psychologist will recognize that idealizing process by which we are all apt to see the friends, the places, the possessions *we* have chosen lit with splendour until, one day, we are forced to see reality and disillusionment sets in. For the moment I saw only sunlight.

4

Las Palmas, like Caesar's Gaul was divided into three parts. First there was the region round the docks where the Sindhi Hindu and Jewish shops flourished, in what the tourist leaflets called enthusiastically 'a shopper's paradise'. 'Whisky, tobacco, still and movie cameras, tape recorders, transistors, watches, everything is cheaper than in the countries of origin.' Unfortunately I had long since tired of the attractions of so-called free ports finding that their only function was to encumber visitors with articles they did not really want, tempted by promises (often false) that they were cheaper than elsewhere. I could buy those iniquitously filthy Canarian cigars which are dressed up to look like Havanas and could only be smoked with minor explosions and patches of black cinders in them, but I could not get a decent cigar for love nor money, or purchase anything useful like stationery at all. From those streets of ugly shops one came to the area of the better-known hotels on a narrow tongue of land which joined the two main cities. Here was the large square known as the Parque Santa Catalina, a plaza surrounded with palm trees and cafés which spilled out over the pavement. This should have been, as it was so persistently advertized to be, an attractive place at night, when it was lit by profuse electricity and crowded with cosmopolitan strollers who could sit under the stars enjoying coffee or cheap drinks, with perhaps a little background music and conversation. But it was not in the least like that. The strollers, regimented families from North Europe, could scarcely be called cosmopolitan, the coffee was of the 'instant' kind and the service, one perspiring waiter for perhaps sixty customers, was execrable. The people, struggling for places at metal tables, had none of the soigné elegance which I had once seen at café tables all over Europe. The perpetual honky-tonk din of juke boxes insulted the night and made all conversations, let alone intelligent or happily frivolous ones, difficult. One spent one's hour there clapping one's hands to attract the attention of an overworked waiter, then pleading with him in order to obtain at last a small measure of dubious whisky in a greasy glass.

But I was determined not to make comparisons with that pleasant Las Palmas of long-ago visits and went on to the third portion of the city, four miles from the docks, which was a busy little metropolis like any of those in provincial Spain which I knew too well.

I remember one evening sitting alone in the Parque, having drunk more Spanish brandy than was good for my health (or according to legend among the British, my eyesight), and trying to imagine the place in the past, before even the reign of Alfonso XIII when I had first seen it, and before the crescendo of noise and business in this midcentury. Even as late as the 1940's before a middle class had been created in Spain, a few swarthy peasants would have saluted members of the colonial aristocracy in their smart carriages, and only a little earlier still in the eighteenth century, hardy British wine shippers had come here to buy Canary Sack and the Spaniards had erected their rococo churches. I tried to imagine yet earlier times when the islands were inhabited by those mysterious people the Guanches who had long since disappeared as a separate race. I sat there amid the din and fuss of the present recalling all I knew of them, learned some thirty years earlier when I had broadcast a 'talk' on the Canary Islands from the British Broadcasting Company's premises on Savoy Hill. The Guanches I read were of the Cro-Magnon type and believed to be an off-shoot of the Berbers; they lived in caves, painted their bodies, wore goat skins and worshipped a god named Acoran. These odd pieces of information about them I remembered and although any reference book would have told me much more, I was, and am, content with them. All that remained of them were some fragments of their language and a few burial grounds and only by an effort of the imagination in a mind hazy with Spanish brandy, could I picture them that evening.

But on the paving-stones of the Parque Santa Catalina not quite all the passers-by were Scandinavian and I met men of several races—Moroccans selling leather poufs and pocket-cases, West Africans with stereotyped paintings and the usual carved figures for which the appetites of tourists seem insatiable, and at last one morning some Europeans, several of whom I had known in Tangier.

5

One of these who perpetually bemoaned his fate, had been called, by one of those fearsome assonant jokes popular in

Tangier 'Mona Lisa', and another was a Russian known as Nicky, who had hung about the Socco Chico with the local bums until he had suddenly inherited a fortune and left Tangier to purchase for himself a large ranch on the island of Lanzarote. Another, here for his health, had been a friend of Joseph's in Delhi when he was a young officer in the British Army while yet another was a Danish giant who had moved from Tangier to the Canary Islands for compulsive reasons. There were also two half-brothers one of whom had been adviser to King Idris of Libya, and two cousins, not Tangerines, named King and Kincaid of Kincaid. There was also a retired naval Commander who had managed to secure a large and comfortable flat. They all knew one another and made just the sort of group of highly individual idlers whom one might have expected to find in the warm climate of the Canary Isles and sitting under the palm trees in the Parque Santa Catalina.

They nearly all had private means of greater or less magnitude and no known occupation beyond walking to the Parque before lunch to purchase their English newspapers and returning to it at night to attempt conversation in the horrendous din about them. They were joined by a phthisic American remittance man and a Chinese masseur from London and finally a retired Consular official who had spent most of his life in the Far East and fascinated me by a lucid exposition of the policies, character and status of Mao Tse Tung. He had discovered a Japanese restaurant in the town and ordered a meal for several of us there. I remember only eating, with difficulty, some raw squid and drinking a pleasant intoxicant, served warm, called *saki* which, said our guide to Japan, was only at its best in the year it was made.

Two among this heterogeneous collection of people had

fallen victims to the wiles of Canarian property dealers whose custom it was to decorate and furnish one flat on the ground floor of a five-storey building and by promising that all the other flats would be exactly like this one when the building was completed, sell the entire block in advance to would-be small investors who were tempted by the prospect of letting their apartments to the Scandinavians in search of the sun. Poor Mona Lisa had been particularly unfortunate through a misunderstanding about the floor-measurements and prospect from the flat he had chosen and purchased for seven or eight thousand pounds. He had waited long and impatiently while the building grew and now found himself with a single narrow passage with a minute bathroom off it. He had been promised a view of the sea from its fifth floor window and it was quite true that by craning out dangerously one could glimpse in one direction a vista of lobster-coloured bodies on the beach, but as the lift and the water supply were both perpetually out of order this eyrie, 'narrow and low and infinitely less' than Mona Lisa had hoped for, filled him with despair.

The other investment had been made by one of the cousins through the giant Dane who was dealing in house property. This one, too, was on the fifth floor and had an erratic lift. It had a fair-sized bedroom and sitting-room and made no pretensions to a pleasing outlook, unless one considered pleasing the prospect of yet another apartment block immediately in front of it which, when completed, would block out not only the sea but the sky. It had been occupied for the year of the owner's possession by a friend of the Dane's who paid no rent and removed any easily movable pieces of the furniture. At last, after months of exasperating Spanish litigation, the tenant had been induced to move out leaving the flat in filth and disrepair. This had happened recently and the owner was willing to clean up the place and let it to me at a suitably low rental. I took it just as Joseph was returning from his holiday in India. This meant at least that I could do some work.

During the years of international house-hunting which I am describing, I lived in some curious places but none which could match this for sheer discomfort and even, as I shall describe, an element of personal danger. But I had not much alternative to that flat and at least it was inexpensive and near the Parque Santa Catalina—for what that was worth—so that I could meet others of the group each morning on my way there to purchase my copy of *The Times* and drink San Patricio, that best of all dry Sherries.

There was also a legacy from the owner—who had not attempted to disguise the disadvantages of the flat—of a simple-minded Canarian who tried to attend to the water-supply, electric light and service of the lift without much success and whose wife came and flicked round daily with a duster. The threat of vertigo prevented me from looking down to the street below from the narrow balcony and the difficulty of climbing the stairs to the fifth floor when the lift was out of order made each descent to the street an anxiety.

But after a few weeks my fortunate facility for turning the most unpromising circumstances into an easy-going routine asserted itself and I rose early, worked for a couple of hours, walked along to the Parque to sit under the palm trees in the company of one or another of that strange little group of people before lunching at a restaurant nearby. This was called El Rayo and though it might be scorned by a gourmet, it was useful for the purposes of a daily lunch, since it had seven 'dishes of the day' served in rotation through the week in a *table d'hôte* lunch which cost 75 pesetas, then about ten shillings. For the six months I remained with Joseph in Las Palmas we must have completed that weekly rota more than twenty times and although it was monotonous, it was never quite unendurable. The place was scrupulously clean, the waiters wore white jackets shining with starch and had clean hands and fingernails. After a time they knew us and welcomed us daily and in turn we knew before arriving in the restaurant what lunch would be served. On Sunday, as in almost every restaurant through the Spanish islands and peninsula, there was *paella*, and although it is a sad fact that the Spaniards have never learned to cook rice, so that Joseph was filled weekly with misgiving, the dish is otherwise not without attraction. On Monday there were *albondigas*, meat-balls served in a rich sauce, and on Tuesday *calamares*, squids, fried in batter or stewed. Wednesday produced a generous *estofado*, (stew) and Thursday braised chicken. Hamburgers came on Friday and veal escallops, thick and not at all Viennese but plentiful, on Saturday. So the week was completed and the rota began again. We both longed for our own cooking but we were never hungry.

During the afternoon I took a siesta and worked again in the early evening, while at night there was nothing to do but go to a bar or the pictures. True, on one or two occasions we watched *pelota basca*, that fast and furious game which came from the Pyrenees and has spread across the world, or went to see a film in Spanish or were invited to a cocktail party by one of the crowd we knew, or on one occasion, never to be repeated by me, were lured into a Spanish discotheque where I was made almost insensible by the continuously ear-splitting noise, but for the rest, the fairly industrious routine I have described turned the weeks into months.

6

There were interruptions and one of them merits recall if any of the minor incidents of this long series of books can be considered to do so.

In the high narrow building of a commercial street in which I had settled each floor was divided into two flats. The door of the lift opened dangerously on the topmost stair and to left and right were narrow doors, my own and that of the neighbours. When I moved in these were already established, a dockland brothel-owner, politely called a cabaret proprietor and his floosy, a plump young woman much given to slopping about the passage in *alpargatas* and a dressing-gown, yawning and smoking black cigarettes. I nodded politely if I met one of them on the stairs or in the lift but did not expect to carry acquaintance further.

One night, returning from the Parque, we found that the flat had been mildly rifled. Some clothes had been taken and a rolled gold lighter of Joseph's. We wondered how entry had been effected and decided that it had been from the roof through the kitchen window. More baffling was how the burglar had escaped since the front door was mortice-locked and had not been broken open. He must have jumped, I decided, from my narrow balcony to that of the neighbours, so that when in the small hours I heard the *burdelero* return I decided to ring at his bell and see whether his flat had been rifled as mine had.

I found him raging and his moll in hysterical tears. They had been robbed and several thousand pesetas had been taken. I told them what had happened to me and explained how I thought the thief had entered and left, but even as I did so I realized that they suspected—or rather, were convinced—that I and Joseph had broken into their flat and taken their money. Foreigners, I could imagine them saying, one of them an oriental, who had only just come to live next door from heaven knew where, having glib explanations for the robbery—it was all too obvious. They were not very intelligent or, except in a special sense, experienced and they were in distress about the loss of their money. I realized that the more I said to convince them the more certain they became that I was guilty so I gave it up, told them to report the matter to the police in the morning and went to bed.

Some uneasy days followed. It seemed that they were unwilling, for one reason or another, to call in the police who fill people of their profession in Spain with apprehension. They rang at my door to ask me to inspect the new lock they had fixed and told me menacingly that if they ever found out who had taken their money they would throw him over the balcony. They watched our comings and goings from the house and asked me whether I had a bank account.

Then one day, just after the early African nightfall, there was a noisy ringing at our bell and I opened the door to find the brothel-keeper, a muscular type, holding a young prisoner in evident distress.

'Here he is!' the man shouted. 'I've caught him on the roof, just about to rob us again. Now what have you to say?'

The question was to me and it became evident that instead of dispelling the Spaniard's suspicions of me the discovery of the youth had only deepened them. He was convinced that I was in league with his captive and had helped him to the roof to rob my neighbours' flat. No kind of reasoning could convince him. He looked from the youth to me and back, expecting to see that we recognized one another and were concealing it.

It appeared when we examined the young man that he

was a Gaditano conscript, serving his time in Las Palmas, and that he had discovered a vantage point on our roof from which he could watch some girls undressing in a flat two streets away. Sex-starved and lonely in the army he had taken to coming here as a more or less innocent *voyeur* and had been caught and seized by my neighbour to answer for the earlier theft from his flat.

It was a ridiculous but a rather tragic situation. I told the *burdelero* that it was quite obvious that the wretched young man, who was now in tears, was speaking the truth and asked him to let him go with a warning not to trespass on our roof again, but as soon as I said this I saw that he became more and more sure that he was dealing with two accomplices. The situation grew tense and ugly and I have no doubt that the Spaniard, if he had had a weapon, would have attacked his compatriot. So I asked Joseph to go down to the Parque and bring one of the policemen who were always on duty there to resolve the impasse. The *burdelero* then said he would not let Joseph out of his sight but would accompany him to the Parque and that meanwhile, on pain of being myself proved guilty, I should keep the youth here.

So I remained in the flat with the unfortunate boy who continued to weep unceasingly. He made no attempt to escape or to persuade me to let him go, to plead or threaten. He simply stood and cried like a small child in terror of grown-ups. I gave him a cigarette and told him I would say what I could for him when the police arrived, but he seemed quite numb and dumb with fear. When Joseph and the *burdelero* returned with a couple of policemen he said little except that he had never stolen anything in his life, or entered any flat in the building and had simply gone up to the roof for something to do. I tried to persuade the police to let him go but the brothel-keeper set up such an outcry about his having been robbed that the police unwillingly led him out. I never saw him again.

But for some unexplicable reason my neighbour's attitude of suspicion was thereafter dropped. His greetings became more civil and he no longer watched our movements. Perhaps he believed he had found the guilty party.

7

I decided to know something of the interior of the island and found an amicable taxi-driver who agreed, for a modest charge to take me up into the hills. We passed through the small sleepy town of Santa Brigada, named not after the patron saint of Ireland, but after Bridget or Birgitta, a remarkable Swedish saint of the fourteenth century. A widow, she took Orders and founded the Order of St Saviour or the Brigittines. As she lived in Rome for the last twenty-three years of her life and made various pilgrimages from there including one to Jerusalem, and as she had known Spain during her early married life, it is conceivable that she came to the Canaries, but more probable that Spanish colonists of a later date had revered her and given her name to a growing village.

From there we climbed by a winding road to the *parador* at Cruz de Trejeda where Joseph and I enjoyed an excellent lunch, one of the few really good meals I had in the Canaries, consisting of roast wild boar prepared in the local fashion. The flesh, sounding so exciting and succulent, is usually dull and rather tasteless, but here the animals live in a semi-wild condition without being specially fed or fattened and the meat is immersed for several days in a potent herbal marinade and has a rich and gamy taste, though it is of the colour of mutton when it is served with cranberry sauce. This was followed by another Canarian speciality *quesadillas* made by filling open pastry tart-cases with a mixture of sugar, sharp goat's cheese, egg, blanched almonds, lemon juice and lemon rind and baked like a lemon curd tart. Excellent.

But our taxi-driver, a good-humoured paterfamilias, knew of something worth finding on this hilltop. He pointed out the twin peaks known as Las Pechas, the breasts, and took us to a point from which we could see the island of Tenerife. But of more interest to me (for I prefer landscapes pictured by painters to the real thing) was a cave in the rocky hillside once inhabited by the Guanches and now the basaltic home of a Canarian shepherd and cheese-maker named Francisco Ramón.

It was no easy task to reach this habitat, dropping from rock to rock like a frolicsome mountain goat, and not many had discovered it except perhaps a few hardy cheese-dealers from the coastal towns. There were two caves, one clean and roughly furnished for Francisco and his wife and semi-idiot daughter, and the other used as shelter for the flock of ewes from whose milk his cheese was made, cheese at every stage of development from the fresh cottage cheese of yesterday to four-kilo monsters made last year. I admit that it may have been the setting and conditions under which it was produced, a cleft in a rocky hillside high above a deep green valley, which made it taste so good, but I do not think it was that. I had eaten raw countrymade cheese in many lands, cheese from the milk of asses, mares, goats, cows, and ewes, but Francisco's surpassed them all. It may be that there is some ambrosial cheese made in a remote region from the milk of llamas, reindeer, camels, yaks, or buffalo and that I may live to eat it. Meanwhile that ewes' milk cheese, made in a cool cave under the scorching Canary sun, had all the purity and flavour that I desire.

We returned by another route passing near the Pico de las Neves and a *mirador* from which the eye ran over the whole panorama of the island. Then to the famous Caldero or Cauldron an almost incredible geological phenomenon, the vast outline of a volcanic crater, many miles across forming a fertile circle of low ground with mountain ranges around it. Then back through the pleasant town of Telde to Las Palmas.

I suppose a journey like that should have made me more reconciled to the dullness of the capital but it did not do so. I realized that the finding of the shepherd's eyrie with its pile of cheeses was a unique experience and that even if I had a car in which to explore every *pueblo* on the island and scan every landscape, this could not lead to a way of life for me. I remembered that other island in the Atlantic of even greater natural beauty and more remarkable vegetation, Madeira, and how it could be encircled by coast road in an afternoon just as La Gran Canaria could be crossed from Las Palmas to Paso de Herrero in a similar time. My feelings, I decided, were quite contrary in this respect to those of my beloved friend Compton Mackenzie, the original of Lawrence's *Man who Loved Islands*. Except when an island is large enough to cease to seem an island, as with Great Britain and Madagascar in my experience, and I feel certain New Zealand and Ireland too, I felt confined and claustrophobic when I was on them, and I was not enough of an archaeologist, geologist or botanist to be satisfied for the rest of my life with the many points of interest to these studies which the Canary Islands presented. I might talk like a misanthrope sometimes, but I knew myself well enough to recognize that *au fond* I was gregarious, a creator and

conserver of friendships, and although I might fleetingly
believe that I could be happy on a beautiful Canarian
mountainside, even if Joseph could stand the solitude, my
natural home for good or ill had to be in a city, even in a
noisy traffic-hustled city like Las Palmas, rather than in the
countryside. It was almost with relief that night that I
walked along to the Parque Santa Catalina, fought for the
possession of a metal chair and awaited the arrival of Mona
Lisa and the rest of them.

8

Among 'the rest of them' was a youngish Englishman
who was in Las Palmas for a curious reason. Two years ago
before the passing of the Sexual Offences Act of 1967 he had
kissed a friend good-night in the seclusion of some trees in
Hyde Park and a prowling police constable had accused him
of impropriety and after some personal abuse had demanded
that he should accompany him to the police-station. No act
which could conceivably be called 'improper' had taken
place and all the constable had been able to say in the
Magistrate's Court to justify his arbitrary act was that the
two men had 'embraced one another in a suggestive way'.
However, those few London policemen who practised this
sort of thing knew their Magistrates and could count on
their respective prejudices, so that no one was surprised
when the Englishman was committed to be tried on a
charge of public indecency.

In Las Palmas he told me the story, recalling that he had
been advised by a solicitor to defend the action, but such
was the opprobrium attached to what were called 'offences'
of this kind that he threw up a good job, parted from his
family and friends and jumped his bail to arrive in the islands

with very little money and not much prospect of employment. He had scraped along somehow, selling advertisement space in English language periodicals which came and went, making small commissions on letting flats and being assisted by other Englishmen. He was now pretty desperate but still refused to return to London. The threats and bullying of the police during the short time he was under arrest had completely unnerved him.

I recall this anomalous and unpleasant incident because it was not uncommon to find exiles like my friend suffering from similar situations prior to the passing of the 'Abse Act'—in Las Palmas, in Tangier, in Majorca, in Malta or in any such refuges on the Mediterranean. Poor Wilde had foreseen this and Lord Arran quoted him on the day when the Second Reading of the Sexual Offences Act secured a majority in the Lords—'My Lords, Mr Wilde was right: the road has been long and the martyrdoms many, monstrous and bloody. Today, please God! sees the end of that road.' Although I believe now, having given considerable study to the subject, that long before the passing of that Act most honourable and self-respecting policemen had tacitly ignored the provisions of the previous laws, yet there were a few, as well I know, who took advantage of them for their own advancement. In some cases this was through ignorance, inherited prejudices, stupidity or jealousy, but in others it was the result of sheer wanton spite, and such men knew where to look for approval and support on the Bench.

These are old unhappy far-off things now and the younger generation find it hard to believe that they happened less than a decade ago, while older victims of them, even now, find themselves with a distrust of the police of all nations which dies hard.

The Canarian police, for instance, were tyrannical in manner if not in practice—at least towards foreigners. To them every long-haired Englishman was a drug-smuggler and every Scandinavian a drunken rowdy. To call at the police station for an extension of a residence permit laid one open to that particular kind of insolence which seems common to the whole profession, worldwide. It was one of the distasteful minor aspects of life in Las Palmas which helped to make me feel restless.

But as one of these aspects arose, another with exactly contrary effect revealed itself. Anna McKew who has appeared in more than one of the books of this series as a creature of loveliness and lovability, my friend then for twelve years or more, decided to visit Las Palmas. It was her custom to spend each winter with her father, Jack Gerber, at his home near Cape Town and as she returned by ship would drop off and spend a week or two with me and Joseph before flying on to London. This seemed to change our whole surroundings. The flat became tolerable, the Parque an amusing meeting-place and the disagreeable things about the city disappeared as Anna with her sanguine temperament, said she was sure I should come to like it better than Tangier and envied us its climate.

She it was who found hitherto undiscovered places of amusement there like a restaurant called the Acuario, an obscure but elegant little place decorated with enormous glass fish tanks in which turtles and a small shark swim about, and the only one that might earn a star in the *Guide Michelin*. It was founded by a Swiss, Hans Egli, and the Canarian head chef was trained in Paris. There was a café kept by an ex-publican from Sussex and his wife where steak-and-kidney pudding was served once a week, and a stretch of open shore not many miles from Las Palmas where one could bathe without being crowded off the beach by Scandinavians. She found a miniature supermarket where English groceries could be bought and she alone of all my friends could threaten me with defeat at Scrabble, a game she played in a manner which I can only call passionate. But when she left for England it seemed that the town grew sultry and dull as it had begun to seem before she came.

9

There was however one more cause for cheerfulness which raised my spirits during the months which would have been Spring if the Canaries had any seasons or changes of climate. It came about through the quite extraordinary memory for minor incidents of the past which I believe I have displayed in this and other books. As I have already recounted, on my way back from Argentina on a German tourist-class liner in 1924 I had gone ashore in Las Palmas with a group of shipboard acquaintances and remained in a Casino half the night. The *Monte Sarmiento* of the Hamburger-Sud Amerikanisch Dampfshiffart Gesellschaft (a multi-syllabic name which I learned to pronounce with unction) was anchored out in the roads and we had been brought ashore by willing oarsmen for a moderate charge per head. They had promised with Castilian oaths of fidelity to wait for us and return us to the ship, and when we reached the docks, being insistently summoned to the ship by sirens, they were there. But now they had changed entirely from the jolly jack tars who had brought us ashore and demanded not twice but three times the sum we had paid before.

Blackmail, we said, with impotent indignation for we were poor, but the continued hooting of the ship's siren seemed to grow more impatient and strengthened their position. At that moment I saw round the neck of one of the spectators who had gathered a tie denoting that its wearer was an Old Tonbridgian, for we were still in the era of significant ties worn by young Englishmen everywhere, club, school, college or regiment.

I addressed the wearer and discovered such details as were commonly exchanged by Old Boys. His name was John Head, he had been in School House when I was a despised dayboy at Tonbridge and he was now working as an engineer with the Grand Canary Coaling Company. Told of our dilemma with the boatmen he intervened as a peacemaker and although he did not persuade them to drop their claim entirely he secured our return to the ship for a sum we could afford.

That argument under the African stars between a young English public schoolboy and some tough Spanish boatmen had taken place more than forty years earlier but I remembered it vividly and when I had to see the British Consul I asked him out of idle curiosity if he remembered a man named Head.

'Remember him?' he said. 'I don't need to remember him. I saw him last night and if you walk along to one of the cafés in the Parque you will see him now, having his elevenses as he does every morning.'

So my hard-worked memory paid off and I found John Head—a more solid and self-assured but none the less recognizable version of the John Head I had met on the docks in 1924 and seen play rugger for the school fifteen during the First World War. He welcomed me back to Las Palmas without, of course, being able to remember me at all and introduced me to a shipowner named Blandy whose family I met in Madeira when I was writing a book about Madeira wine. This one of the Blandy clan was in charge of the family shipping interests in Las Palmas and had the admirable habit of giving caviare parties every Sunday morning before lunch. He surprised me (as I am always surprised and delighted when this happens) by being a habitual reader of my books which by another good extravagance of his he purchased on a monthly list from London, a splendid patron to have. I spent some happy hours at those sabbatarian parties at which the caviare was of the large red globular kind and offered unstintingly, and met a number of charming people who almost convinced me that Las Palmas, which we viewed from the windows of Blandy's house overlooking it from green heights, was a place in which I could settle.

But this impression vanished when I descended to the suicidal streets of badly driven motor-cars, the over-crowded beaches and uninteresting food, and the perpetual bargaining of the free port. Before May had begun to mark nearly half a year's residence in the Canary Isles I had become convinced that it was not the place in which I wanted to spend the remaining years of my life and by June I had decided to move on. I still had the illusion that there were plenty of places as welcoming, inexpensive and interesting as Tangier had been when I first found it, for I was a long way yet from realizing that apart from my own approaching senescence the western world had lost much of its charm while I had been in my Rip Van Winkle hide-out in Tangier. I still thought I had before me merely the small problem of finding the right place for a home and resolved to look elsewhere.

A minor irritation was the want of any kind of local cuisine. It was unbelievably difficult to obtain any fish in Las Palmas and what shellfish was found in the restaurants had been imported from Galicia. Meat, as usual in Spanish territories, was tough and chickens were reared by battery-feeding and consequently tasteless. There was no game.

There is a local wine but Ben Jonson, who wrote, 'But that which most doth take my Muse and me, Is a pure cup of rich Canary wine,' might now find it somewhat thin, and Keats would not again ask, 'Have ye tippled drink more fine Than mine host's Canary wine?' Wine, bananas, tomatoes, and a few other vegetables and fruits are produced here in exportable quantities. But where are the Canary dishes?

This proved to be a difficult question to answer. The earliest known inhabitants of the islands seem to have been unenterprising in the matter of food and to have subsisted largely on *gofio*, a substance still popular today. In simple terms, *gofio* is a coarse flour milled from toasted maize or sometimes toasted wheat. It is a light khaki colour and has a taste of its own, which strangers either take to with enthusiasm or abhor. As an uncooked paste it is eaten by the old-fashioned Canarians instead of bread with certain dishes, a spoonful or two added to *café con leche* makes the national breakfast. *Gofio* biscuits are made from eggs, bananas, wheat flour, *gofio*, salt, sugar, chopped nuts, and oil. *Gofio* flour may also be sprinkled over stews and soups, as the Italians use grated cheese. It is so truly, and indeed almost exclusively, of the islands that one hears the expression, '*El es mas canario que gofio de trigo*,'—he is more Canarian than wheat *gofio*.

Two simple but too piquant sauces that belong essentially to the Canary Islands are *mojo rojo* and *mojo verde*. The first is too fiery for human consumption, the second, less peppery but perhaps more palatable is eaten with rabbit or kid if either of these could by any means be obtained. *Mojo rojo* and *mojo verde* are best described as relishes and are made fresh for each meal. The ingredients of *mojo rojo* include garlic, cuminseed, sweet red peppers or paprika, salt, pepper, chili peppers, oil, and vinegar. For *mojo verde* coriander seeds and parsley are substituted for the cuminseed and chili peppers. The dry ingredients are pounded in a mortar to a fine powder. The peppers are then crushed in the mortar and combined with the dry mixture, oil and vinegar into a thick liquid the consistency of ketchup.

I did not give up the search for Canarian dishes without a struggle and drove out to inland towns and restaurants. Among those I sampled were several soups and stews. *Potaje canario*, a hearty vegetable concoction, is eaten all over the islands by rich and poor. Its components vary according to income, available ingredients, and taste. The preparation begins with a good meat stock. A *fritura* (tomatoes, garlic, and onions fried to a mush in oil) and some squares of fairly fatty bacon or salt pork that have been fried separately are added to the stock. White beans or chick-peas, pumpkin, green beans, carrots, corncobs, potatoes, cabbage or spinach leaves, and fried shredded onions (any or all of these may be used) go in next, and the soup is cooked for about twenty minutes. It is served in very large plates or bowls, often with pieces of marrow. Two varieties of *potaje canario* are *sopa de berro* and *sopa de rabanos*. In the former potatoes and watercress are the only vegetables used; in the latter radish leaves are substituted for the watercress.

Pescado asado al horno (fish baked in the oven) is a peasant dish found all over the Iberian Peninsula but often with the fish in fillets rather than whole, which spoils the generous effect. A large baking dish is lined with slices of tomato and onion, a little chopped parsley, a couple of garlic cloves, and enough oil to cover the vegetables. On this bed is placed any large fish, cleaned and scored but not skinned or beheaded, then more slices of onion and tomato. The fish is baked for twenty or forty minutes according to its size and served in the baking dish, garnished with slices of lemon. A sauceboat of *mojo rojo* is passed round.

But none of this added up to a cuisine and even more lacking on the island were other forms of culture, music, painting or any conversation more significant than the gossip and small talk which rattled continuously at the café tables in the Parque.

10

There was, however, as I discovered that summer, a meeting place for young refugees, hippies, and other flotsam chiefly from the British Isles. They were the first young men of this kind I had met for in Tangier the hippies were mostly American and were quickly expelled to Spain as having no visible means of support. I found them interesting and in many ways likeable.

They had discovered and adopted a little working men's bar with a zinc counter and no seating which was not far from the Parque and here they met, coming and going for short or long periods as the strange contingencies of their life dictated. They smoked pot continuously but so far as I could discover used no hard drugs. A few of them were adorned with ugly facial growths, moustaches and beards particularly, and nearly always side-burns. Their talk was unreal but imaginative and I learned from two teenage brothers from Sussex, who in another epoch would have been farm-labourers satisfied with a game of darts in the local pub, that they had already been into Nepal and were on their way to an island off the American coast given by one of the Beatles to a colony of their kind.

But they all had surprising qualities. They invited me, a

much older man who was interested but could not share their way of life to join in their counsels without reserve, and they refused to accept more drink from me than from any of themselves. Their manners were agreeable, the warmth of their comradeship touching and their natural intelligence (by which I do not mean such nonsense as IQ rating) was high. One or two girls came and went among them who were neither offensively being 'chaps' nor girlishly flirtatious but sympathetic and unassuming. They lived irrespective of sex three or four to a room in doss-houses near the docks but in person and habit they were scrupulously clean. I was attracted to them all, boys and girls, and was heartbroken when suddenly, moved by some secret impulse, they made a mass exodus from the island, concealing themselves or bribing their way on board small trading vessels.

If this, I remember saying to myself, is what all the fuss is about concerning the younger generation, their anti-social behaviour and drug-taking, there was little to worry us. They had made a way of life for themselves which might be called dissolute and idle (though they told me they worked furiously at intervals to accumulate enough money for more travels), but as human beings dissolute or not, I at least found them lovable and worth while. I did not know it then, but it would be four or five years before I met their kind again.

Their departure left such a gap that I discussed with Joseph the immediate prospect of finding another home and before the end of June we set out on a new venture. I intended to *try* (I emphasize the word), Gibraltar. Like so many other places in that long trek it could in theory provide a quite possible dwelling. I knew it well by coming across from Tangier for shopping and believed its climate was much the same as on the African coast. Although my friend Darrell Bates had been appropriately knighted and retired from the Secretariat, I had a number of friends in Gibraltar including the First Minister, Sir Joshua Hassan and a miracle-working physician and surgeon Dr Giraldi. There were I believed, television programmes there and so far as I knew at that time I could cross to Algeçiras on the ferry and of course to Tangier on the *Mons Calpe*. Communication with U.K. by mail, telephone, ship and plane was convenient and after the limitations of shopping in Las Palmas it would be good to have Lipton's within reach. I might suffer from claustrophobia, I conceded, but I knew there was one of the best English libraries in Europe.

Moreover I heard from John Head that the last of the liners from South Africa which had once called habitually at both Las Palmas and Gibraltar on its way to England would arrive in ten days' time with a couple of vacant cabins. That clinched it and I booked our passages, since I was not yet reconciled to the idea of flying and in any case we had far too much baggage with us for that. So on an early summer morning just six months after I had come ashore I went with Joseph down to the docks to leave Las Palmas—so far as one can predict in an uncertain life—for good.

Three

Gibraltar

Throughout my life my vagrant route seems to have crossed the by-paths of history on more occasions than should have been my share. I met a minor revolt in Uruguay on my way to Buenos Aires as a youth, witnessed the abdication of Alfonso XIII of Spain and like most Englishmen was involved in the Spanish Civil War a few years later. I left Vienna a week before Hitler entered it in 1938, was in Germany at the time of the abominable 'crystal night' which marked the end of all restraint in the persecution of the Jews, and in Bombay when Gandhi and Nehru were arrested in 1943. In London I watched the birth pangs of the Welfare State immediately after the War, and have heard firing in the Champs Elysées during what has been euphemistically called 'unrest' at the same period. I was in Morocco when it was declared independent and in Dublin for the burning down of the British Embassy in 1972.

None of these succeeded in making me feel wholly concerned in these issues and I have always maintained that the novelist's (and perhaps also the autobiographer's) concern is not with politics or religion except as the raw material of story-telling, a point of view exactly opposite to that of H. G. Wells who scorned his own considerable talents in literature and maintained that it was his duty to put politics above prose so that he lectured mankind when he could have been creating more fiction as splendid as *Kipps* and *Mr Polly*. But there have been at least five public events during the years of my own manhood which have made me a partisan. In the General Strike of 1926 I incurred, for the only time on a political issue, the anger of my father. I was alone in feeling as I did, both in my immediate surroundings and among my family and friends. I recognized this then and thereafter as a solitary creed which could never be shouted in happy unison with fellow believers, for thus it would lose its essence. Held in common with others it becomes its very antithesis—a movement or a conspiracy.

When the strike was 'settled'—that was the word—I felt even more bitterly convinced, for the dirty trick I had foreseen was only too apparent. The owners had stood their ground, Baldwin by a masterpiece of prevarication and a slimy appeal to the nation had not only got his own way but added to his stature in public esteem, the Union leaders had abandoned the miners' cause, at least sufficiently to call off the strike, and my imaginary mining community was left rather worse off than before its first demands were made. To hell with them, I said, to hell with all politicians and conference men, all makers of guarded promises, all time-servers and skipjacks, all who look for compromise and pacification. The miners might have been unjustified in the first place for all I knew or cared; they had been sold down the river by a lot of solemn monkeys talking in London, a blackguardly breach of faith.

Then at the time of the abdication of King Edward VIII my attitude was, I like to think, no less ahead of its time and formed entirely by myself, for I was in Buenos Aires and away from all home influences. And I found that hatred can be a wonderfully illuminating thing. If I had not felt for Baldwin what I did, I might not have realized that the King was being jockey'd out of his kingdom by a time-server seeking his own popularity, exactly as the miners had been humbugged by the same smirking functionary with similar tactics ten years earlier.

In the days of the Munich Crisis I was no less committed but my identification with any party was far less clear-cut. I caused some indignation when thirty years after it happened I wrote in *The Sound of Revelry*, 'Perhaps no event in history has led to more boastful hindsight than this, more claims to have seen the folly and wickedness of appeasement. It is all very well to talk of Guilty Men and to see in the wretched Chamberlain a credulous and cowardly old temporizer who betrayed us. We were all (or very nearly all) guilty men and should have the courage to admit it. The rapturous crowds at the airport who cheered him hysterically as he waved that ridiculous piece of paper were not exceptional people—they cheered for all but a tiny minority of not necessarily wiser Britons.' Among them, I had to own, myself.

I did not face any kind of dilemma two years later when France had fallen. It was only a question of which branch of which Service I should join, and that was not a political question at all, but at the end of the war I felt I was, though impotently, in the political lists again over the question of India and believed then, as I do still, that Clement Attlee proved himself a great man when without further temporizing or condition-making he sent Mountbatten to Delhi to relieve us at once of the intolerable shame and horror which would have ensued if we had tried to remain.

Mine had not then been a very noble or perspicacious record as a political thinker but at least it was an individual and an honest one, free from self-deceit. It had been even more uncertain over the Spanish Civil War when I was consumed with dislike for those few Englishmen, on both sides of the fence, who seemed to seek publicity for themselves in the situation, and I expressed this far too grandiloquently in the Preface I wrote for Colonel Casado's book *The Last Days of Madrid*.

I reached Gibraltar just in time for small but significant events, a miniature crisis which compared as a personal experience with the more important ones I had known. On the very Sunday on which we came ashore the ferry linking Gibraltar with Spain ran across Algeçiras Bay for the last time and as the land frontier was already closed this meant the end of all connection with the mainland. Several thousand workers who were employed on the Rock would go back to the Spanish coastal towns for the last time and Gibraltar would be left—for a time at least—without labour, without fresh food, and without the cheerful Andalucian faces which had been seen in its streets for so long. The British who lived or spent holidays in Gibraltar could no longer cross to the mainland to seek relief from the appalling monotony or enjoy the entertainments, feeble though they were but welcome to the British servicemen, of the scruffy little town of La Linea.

Realization of what all this would mean became a matter of concern on that very day and was brought home to me within an hour of landing by a barman in my hotel who had worked there for fifteen years and would have to catch the last ferry back that afternoon and search for a job in

Algeçiras. For the following days there was chaos in the town—no waiters or cooks in the hotels and restaurants, no stall-holders or produce in the market, no assistants in the shops and no workers in the dockyard. Gibraltar had begun a campaign in Britain to bring holiday-makers here and this, ironically, had been successful so that hotels were crowded with tourists who could only with the greatest difficulty be fed and had to make their own beds and do their own washing. The cinema operators had, fortunately, been brought from home so that programmes could continue and the recently opened Casino kept open. Enough of the pubs and fish-bars were owned and run by Britons or Gibraltarians to continue serving, but the flamenco singers and dancers who had produced frenzied music in the cafés and night-clubs were heard no more.

As if by common consent almost none of these facts appeared in the London Press, for it was universally agreed that the Spaniards should be denied the satisfaction of knowing that they had temporarily crippled the life of the Peñon which they so much coveted. There were reports about the half-hearted attempts made by Spain to interrupt the air services and accounts of the sufferings of labourers in Spain who had lost their jobs and become, many of them, deprived of their livelihood. There was much talk of the loyalty of Gibraltarians and how they would suffer any inconvenience or shortage rather than yield to the blandishments of Spain. There were even rhapsodies about the island fastness and comparisons with Great Britain when it had been left to face the Nazis alone in 1940.

This was not all nonsense or propaganda. Gibraltar did, and does still refuse to become a province of Spain and nowhere (except perhaps in Ulster) is the Union Jack so prominently and defiantly displayed. Everyone, British and

Gibraltarian alike, showed ingenuity and determination in coping with the difficulties of having lost its entire labour force at a stroke. Advertisements appeared in the British Press for students, male and female, who wanted to work for holiday money on the Rock and slowly the restaurants and cafés were manned by hairy-faced young amateurs who showed a great deal of willingness if not much natural aptitude. Hairdressers appeared, chefs were lent to the restaurants by the Army Catering Corps and vegetables and fruit were bought in Morocco and shipped across on the *Mons Calpe* together with a number of workers of somewhat anomalous experience. The holiday-makers grumbled through their package fortnights and departed and the wheels began slowly to turn again.

None of these minor inconveniences affected me very much. I had Joseph to deal with most of them and was accustomed to improvising comfort. What did hit me and made me see at once that Gibraltar as a home was impossible was their basic cause—the final and irrevocable closing of the frontier with Spain. Gibraltar, when one could run across to eat and drink and visit friends on the Spanish mainland was small and uninviting enough, but now when it could not be left except to go to Africa it was impossible. But I had to be convinced of that before I moved farther afield.

2

Gibraltar had been more than a mere shopping centre to me during my years in Tangier. My friend Darrell Bates had been Colonial Secretary there which meant in practical terms the head of the whole civil service and thus all the civil affairs of the Colony under the Governor who represented the Queen. Darrell and Susan his wife had been dear friends of mine during most of my years in Tangier and with counsel and hospitality had seen me through a couple of personal crises. I remember how one Sunday Susan had unexpectedly arrived at my Tangier flat to stay the day. Her coming was explained when the Sunday newspapers arrived and I saw that Darrell had received his knighthood on the previous day. Susan had felt that the rush of congratulations in Gibraltar would have been too much for her and had sought my home as a temporary hide-out. It had not occurred to me before that—a fact which should stir Women's Lib to hysteria—the wife of a prominent citizen being honoured becomes Lady So-and-So, whether she likes it or not. Susan was delighted for Darrell's sake but had no particular wish to be Lady Bates herself. I suppose silly alternatives could be devised, like 'Sir Darrell and Mrs Susan Bates' but they were beyond the terms of reality and would bring both themselves and the distinction offered by the Queen into ridicule.

So Darrell and Susan until they had departed into retirement in England had provided a refuge when I was in Gibraltar and although they rarely discussed local affairs I had become interested in these. It was therefore an additional loss, which I realized in my first days of return, that I knew no compatriots on the Rock and should have to find a home and create a way of life unaided and without the advice of residents.

The Rock Hotel was full, largely with senior officers and their wives who were feeling the loss of all domestic service in the town as their Marias and Carmens and Emilias had departed tearfully on the last ferry. I found a hotel in which a few score tourists from the northern counties of England were 'facing the crisis', at first with good humour when it seemed rather a lark but with increasing indignation when

amateur cooks were all that could be found and their meals
(for which they had paid in advance) were unpunctual and
inadequate.

There were indignant meetings in the lounge, talk of the
cruelty of enticing people to holiday abroad when there was
not adequate provision for them and desperate anxiety about
what the next meal would be. The proprietor or manager
solved this by the discovery that fish and chips which were
imported from England for the shops in the town, could
be purchased ready cooked and re-heated in the kitchens,
and that as an alternative the manufactured small meat pies
which had become a feature of English pubs were also
obtainable. With these two the guests were, it appeared, not
merely satisfied but delighted and congratulated one
another on the fact that it was 'just like being at home'.

I found these conversations and the mixture of the
Dunkirk spirit of my compatriots with discontent about the
hotel, somewhat depressing and looked for somewhere else
in which to stay. I found that there were two tall apartment
blocks at the foot of Main Street, one of them of fair-sized
flats overlooking the yacht harbour and the sea designed for
officers and their families or other retired gentlepeople who
wanted to remain here after years of service in Gibraltar,
the other consisting of tenements for Gibraltarian workers.
Among the 'gentlemen's residences' there were a number of
expensive flats to be let furnished during the holiday season,
their purchasers profiting by being absent for the summer
months. The cheapest of these, with a skeleton supply of
furniture, would cost me £20 a week and since there was
no alternative on the whole of the Rock I took it and
obtained the necessary sheets, blankets and cutlery from the
Naafi through one of those universal providers whom one
meets in garrison towns usually in the local bars. So at least

C

now I could work again and set out to finish *Exiles*, the novel about Tangier on which I was engaged.

3

I did not remain solitary for long. Among the characteristics I recognized in myself when, a couple of years later, a heart attack and a subsequent period of convalescence gave me time and opportunity for contemplation, was that I have always been dependent for happiness and interest on the friendship of both men and women and that these have been (for me) divided into two kinds—the simple, extrovert, usually not highly educated younger folk with whom I am on terms of instant understanding and often affection, and those with whom on less commonplace, sometimes even intellectual subjects I like to converse. (I think also that those who attract me sexually belong exclusively to one or the other of these two categories, but that is another and less interesting matter.)

So it was now as the weeks began to pass in Gibraltar, I made friends with two young ex-Naval ratings of an adventurous, even mildly villainous, turn of ambition, called, but I cannot say whether christened, Mike and Steve and their highly entertaining friends. On the other hand there was a truly remarkable man of the world, brilliant and experienced in many matters, whose delightfully oriental and biblical name, Joshua Hassan, had at once excited my interest when I had met him in the home of Darrell and Susan Bates. Sir Joshua Hassan, CBE, MVO, QC, to give him his full title, was Chairman of the Legislative Council of Gibraltar and commonly known as First Minister. He was also an able lawyer, called to the Bar, Middle Temple. He had advised me professionally and drawn my Will, which was a simple document leaving the little I possessed to Joseph. With him, now that Darrell and Susan had gone, I enjoyed the only materially worthwhile conversation I had on the Rock and used to lunch with him and his charming second wife, on frequent occasions. That was all the mental or social recreation I knew except when friends came across from Tangier, Anna McKew and Trish Wilton or my publisher Jeffrey Simmons of W. H. Allen who came from London to discuss the progress of *Exiles* of which we both had great hopes.

There was, it is true, a television station on the Rock, but its emissions consisted mostly of potted black-and-white programmes made in Australia or the States, with once a week a variety show for an hour from London. The presentation and announcing were amateurish and there was an awkward air of 'Well, we're doing our best', about the whole thing which often made it embarrassing to watch.

There was also a Casino which had been opened after a great deal of controversy a couple of years before. But somehow *roulette* with English *croupiers* and played with British currency seemed in some way uninviting, perhaps because I was not a committed gambler and only enjoyed green cloth games of chance as part of continental holidays— never in any place which was even temporarily my home, probably because I was instinctively afraid of becoming an addict. Astrological wiseacres had told me that being born under the sign of Gemini I should be lucky at *roulette* and it was true that I had hit patches of success at game in Montevideo in 1937 and at Pau in 1948, but if I had been guided by this kind of superstition it would have been disastrous and money cost me too much in labour for me to have the courage or abandon of a natural gambler. Besides

I did not like the Gibraltar Casino which lacked the professionalism I had found in other homes of gambling.

Then there were cinemas and as I have confessed in these books I have at different times in my life been utterly devoted to films and even had periods of daily cinema-going. I find it hard to believe that anyone who has grown as I have from the days of Max Sennet silent films to this period of X certificates can have enjoyed a full life or exercised his imagination without what was undoubtedly the most vital and revealing art of the first half of the twentieth century. Which is a big way of saying that I am a buff of the silver screen and delight in not having missed any of the significant or even the most publicised films of my time. Of these there was shown during those weeks in Gibraltar a haunting picture about drug-taking named *The Valley of the Dolls* with incidental music which frightens me today, as the music in the opening sequences of *Midnight Cowboy* rang in my ears for years. I am a natural victim of the make-believe of the cinema and can go along with any plot, any incredible coincidence, any unlikely circumstance, so long as the film has that mysterious quality by which it turns its viewers to children greedy for the next moment. Animated cartoons do not tax any credulity nor the dramas of science fiction. I believe in the premises of the makers of Western and American war films, even in the postulates of French farce if I am in any way allowed to do so.

It might be concluded from this that on the several occasions—one of which occurred during my stay in Gibraltar—on which I have sold film rights of a novel of mine, I must have been eager to participate in its adaptation for the screen. Not so. I have sufficient respect for the makers of films to know that the originator of an idea which has been developed as fiction has no place in its adaptation to this very different form of art and I find foolish and self-deceiving in a writer that kind of vanity which insists on allowing no detail or aspect of his story to be changed, since after all the making of a film does not change the book he has written. I have been fortunate in receiving several sums from producers who wish to use work of mine, but the only time I have worked on a set was for a film made in English, French and Spanish from a short story by Stendhal.

All this may explain why on several evenings a week during that period in Gibraltar I found my way to one of the two cinemas then functioning and walked back to my flat through the tiresome streets.

4

Life devolved into routine again, but it was an even less eventful routine than in Las Palmas. The flat faced across the bay and at night the lights of La Linea shone mockingly. Immediately below us was a yacht club and a great coming and going of pleasure boats. But the most notable thing in that flat was the repetition of the screaming din of planes landing and taking off from the airport only a hundred or two yards away, an offensive and merciless sound. The sound of aircraft always seems to have something malign and aggressive in it, as though it is a warcry of scorn to all who want to live in peace. Blast you, says its deafening roar, blast you and your little cosy homes, we have work to do in the air, the unremitting tasks of fetching and carrying. We care absolutely nothing for you or your sensitive ears or your wish to think, work, read or listen to music. We are almighty and we mean to continue screeching over your head or landing near your homes to the end of time. So fuck you, Jack, we're all right.

I knew, as I was awakened sweating by that stentorian mechanized thunder, that even if Gibraltar had no more disadvantages than this I should have to leave it before the summer was over and I felt genuine sympathy with house-holders everywhere who have had to suffer this torment.

I went for a week to Tangier which I had left less than a year before but it seemed already unfamiliar. Anna McKew gave a party for me but I felt guilty and disturbed at the people I had known for so long, perhaps because I was even then in the course of painting comic portraits of some of them in my novel *Exiles*. Back in Gibraltar I could still find nothing to do except when I was working or going with Joseph up the single street which *is* the town on foraging expeditions to find something to eat except groceries.

The public library was something of a refuge and the librarian liked my books and there was a sizeable row of them. It had pleasant reading-rooms open to the patio and a garden behind the building and it must have been—and I daresay remains to this day—the only public library in which you could ring for a drink and enjoy a whisky and soda as you gathered data from reference books.

There were other traditional sights and customs in Gibraltar, the famous Barbary apes and the weekly Changing of the Guard outside the Governor's house and names like Monkey's Alamada, O'Hara's Tower and Rock Gun. But after my time in India in the last years of the Raj, these anachronisms and the excessively proclaimed patriotism of the people did not stir me.

While I was still there elections for membership of the Legislative Council, of which Joshua Hassan was Chairman, were held in the town and by a piece of skullduggery or tacit anti-Semitism by some of the local shopkeepers, or through his own over-confidence or negligence, he failed to get a majority, which threw the whole place into confusion. He seemed not at all concerned for himself and told me that he was glad to be able to have some time for his own work, but he was (like everyone of intelligence who cared about that strange little colony) very much concerned with what might befall Gibraltar.

The unhappy decision was of course reversed at the next election and he is now back in office. But throughout the last stifling months of my stay on the Rock this was yet another cause for my decision to leave.

5

What, I ask myself somewhat impatiently today did I—or for the matter of that do I—think about 'the Gibraltar Question'.

First like the problems of Kashmir and Ulster, and for very much the same reasons, it is intractable and probably at least in our time insoluble. It has the same elements as these western and eastern questions, the problems of two sets of people differing in religion and culture, each of which deeply and honestly believes it has right on its side and each blind to the other's point of view.

Dignity may not be much of a yardstick by which to judge the conduct of nations but it must be admitted that both Britain and Spain have shown the most deplorable lack of it in their dealings over this.

The British have the nine points of possession and sit complacently on the Rock, secure in their defences. They took up their position there by right of conquest, and they hold it by force of arms. Whether we like the admission or not we keep Gibraltar against the Spanish claims, rightful or otherwise, by strength, and strength alone and justify it by arguments which depend on history and law, and not on today's considerations of justice or generosity. We quote old treaties, deride hispanic attempts to make a case and show no sympathy for the frenetic patriotism of Spain which has suddenly awoken to the anomaly of having a foreign power in occupation. Tories laugh at the possibility of giving up 'Gib—the bastion of the Mediterranean', though the more intelligent of them admit that its military value is minimal if it exists at all. British Socialists take another line and one which may recoil against them in the future. How, they ask, can we contemplate 'handing over' thirty thousand British freedom-lovers to the Fascist State of Spain? Though neither of the two categories could be convincingly justified by the facts, they are lulled by their self-righteousness and still believe that the Spanish Civil War was a struggle between the Fascist murderers on one side and brave Democrats on the other.

Spain, on her side, has been guilty of some sillier breaches of taste and reason in her efforts to make herself heard. She has let her authoritarian press be exposed to world ridicule by the hysterical commentary on the subject by its writers, and shown the feebleness of her case by appealing to the so-called Decolonization Committee of the United Nations knowing that its members would accept any argument to annoy one of the great powers. She has indulged in petty and dangerous gestures like sending a coal-burning gunboat near the Gibraltarian coast to befoul the air, trying (and failing) to harass civilian aircraft using the runway constructed ingeniously over the water, moving her customs post nearer to our own on the road between Gibraltar and La Linea, raving about British royal visits to the Rock and withdrawing her labour force from the dockyards without being able to absorb the men of that force into any local industry.

So the two sides haggle and abuse one another and only a rather childish kind of pride is served by either of them.

6

Where next? Since I still refused to fly and had no intention of returning to England, I consulted the shipping agents and was informed that one of the few passenger ships calling at Gibraltar during the rest of that year would leave in four weeks' time bound for Greece and Cyprus.

Well, why not?

Four

Cyprus

For the voyage of several days' duration on a Greek ship I engaged first class accommodation. I could not afford this extravagance but easily made myself believe that it would be worth the difference, that an outside state-room on an upper deck would save me and Joseph from dark and poky cabins in what the cliché always calls the bowels of the ship and that the food would be very much better. Perhaps. The cabins on the lower decks were full to overflowing with American Jewish passengers on their way to Israel for the celebrations of that year (1969) and they formed queues for their dining room at each meal. It was not, in any case, an enjoyable voyage for there was no port of call between Gibraltar and Piraeus.

Then, of all absurdities, we had one day and night in Athens before a smaller ship would take us East to Cyprus, one day in which to visit the Acropolis, to see all those things about which I had read since I had managed to reach the classical Lower Fifth and heard H. R. Stokoe drone out his lists of Greek irregular verbs. I had never been a good classical scholar but I had given so many hours to the painful study of Greek, which was taught unimaginatively at Tonbridge as at most English public schools, that I felt I should be rewarded with at least a glimpse of the marvels of Athens, and begin to become acquainted with its atmosphere, buildings and people. I belonged to the Western end of the Mediterranean, a fact which would become more and more insistent in my mind as I lived in Cyprus, but at least I ought to have gained some knowledge of Greece, if it was only from a tourist's sightseeing.

But time and tide gave me no chance. My passage was booked on the ferry boat running from Piraeus to Limassol and next morning I had to leave with only a craving ambition to spend months in Athens and know 'the rudiments of Paradise', an ambition which today still remains unfulfilled.

We came ashore in Limassol on a hot evening in September and persuaded a taxi to load up our large pile of baggage and drive to the nearest hotel. These instructions seemed to amuse the taxi-driver, a stocky English-speaking Cypriot, who said we should be lucky if we found any hotel, near or far, with accomodation to let. It was not yet the end of the season and Limassol was crowded. However, he would try. Two hours later with all but two of the possible hotels approached in vain, exhausted and thirsty, we came to one on the outskirts, set among pines and surrounded with flower-beds, where the proprietor received us with consideration, indeed with generosity. He had no accommodation. Why hadn't we written to book rooms? But we must come in and have a drink while he saw what he could arrange for us somewhere else.

This I came to know was typical of Cyprus. It is an island

of extremes, in climate and character. We had suffered two hours of surly, sometimes hostile refusals from other hotels, of fatigue and near despair, and in a moment we now found ourselves at a table in the garden enjoying drinks for which the owner was genuinely anxious not to receive payment, while he telephoned to every place of possible accommodation he knew. There were English people at other tables some yards from us and they seemed to be enjoying their dinner and their Cypriot wine. Our view of the whole island was suddenly transformed so that it had become a friendly and delightful place. This, too, we should know in the months ahead was one of the characteristics of Cypriots, seeming volatility, sudden extremes of mood so that rises and falls in one's spirits were forever at work.

The hotel-owner, having decided to befriend us, could not be deflected from his purpose. He telephoned again and again and sent members of his staff on mysterious missions. He came out to us in the garden at intervals to regret that this or that hope had failed but that he was now trying another. He would find us *something*, he promised.

At last he did. There was, he said, a small hotel in the town—well, hardly a hotel, an inn or boarding-house rather, where they could let us one room. It was not, he said at once, the sort of place he could recommend. We should not find it very comfortable. But it was all there was and at least we could stay the night and perhaps find better accommodation in the morning. It was not in a 'good' street, but among the night-clubs and such. The people might not be very refined. He was sorry that he had not been able to do better for us. But perhaps we would like to try it?

Not in the least alarmed, indeed rather attracted by this prospect we drove through the neglected narrow streets of the town to the promised resting-place, and in a way it fulfilled all our hopes.

It was not, to be fair, a brothel. It would better be described as a dormitory established for whores. Its owner had owned a large open-air night-club and cabaret and had opened a small hotel across the road to house the girls who were politely called his *artistes*. The night-club had been closed because of some disagreement between the waiters' union and the owner's son who ran the place, but the hotel remained open and the young man and his mother received me and Joseph and offered us a large room with two beds and a low ceiling which even on that evening was stiflingly hot and fuggy.

The hotel consisted of what would be called in a German inn a *gessellschaft zimmer*, an all-purpose room which was a café open to the street, a dining-room for the residents and a sitting-room for the proprietors. We breakfasted there each morning, glad to escape at an early hour from our airless bedroom, lunched there, dined at night, and spent any of the time there when we were not out of doors, reading newspapers and conversing with all comers.

It had infinite variety. The ladies who were of many races would intrigue and quarrel among themselves, try out pieces of clothing or jewelry which they had come by and criticize these on others. New faces would appear and disappear among them and tragedies recounted—how one had not her fare to escape from Cyprus to Beirut, a city which attracted them all, how another's bruises had been caused by an angry client on the night before, and how good or bad were their 'acts' since most of them made some pretence at performances in other *boîtes de nuit*. I came to know most of their names and receive their confidences, but the stories they told, though I daresay quite truthful, so much resembled old-fashioned fiction about *demi-mondaines* in Paris which had been in print a thousand times from the novels of Leonard Merrick onwards, that they were of no direct use to me.

May I be permitted an interpolation about this? I distrust and dislike the layman's idea that an author is perpetually searching for stories of this or any other kind and I simply do not believe that Somerset Maugham's short stories of the East were based on 'plots' gathered for him from tea-planters by Gerald Haxted, according to the timeworn myth. I at any rate always have more ideas than I can ever find time to develop and interpret as fiction and I thank no one for burdening me with the story of his life in order to provide me with 'copy'.

But recalling here something of what I saw and overheard of those girls is another matter. One of them had secured a young Cypriot boy-friend and astonished us all by announcing the date on which she was to be married in church. Her wedding-presents followed, each displayed to every one of us who responded with congratulations. The young man himself arrived and there were long sessions at a table in a corner between the fiancées, watched, but not interrupted. The happy auguries of this affair seemed to displease only one of the congregation, a big cynical girl with pursed lips who was determined to ridicule it all and treated the bride-to-be with mocking incredulity, explaining to me and the rest that if we really thought the marriage would take place we were crazy. Whether it did or not I shall never know for the young man arrived one day in a motor-car, bundled his sweetheart into it and drove away. Neither of them were seen by any of us again.

Some sensation was caused by the arrival of a young homosexual six-footer with bright yellow curly hair. He travelled with a pretty German girl and with her did a double strip-tease act in a neighbouring cabaret. He spoke English in the unmistakable manner of one brought up in a working-class family in the Home Counties but claimed to be Argentine.

He might have interested Harford Montgomery Hyde who wrote a homosexual case-book called *The Other Love*, full of knowing details, but he had nothing much to say to me. All he wanted was to get a booking in Beirut or Tripoli. 'The Arabs are so wonderful,' he said with a leer. 'I love working there. They never leave anyone alone for a minute! I could tell you some stories about them!' and his long, rather beautiful body waved about like a sapling in the wind. 'I suppose they're dangerous but I don't care. I often say, if you're afraid you'll never get anywhere. They are a bit cruel but I *like* that!'

I asked him about his German partner and he pouted. 'She's greedy, my dear,' he said. 'Always trying to take someone away from me. But I can look after myself. Particularly with Arabs. They always want me!'

There were other characters who spent most of their days in the general room of the hotel, one of them a tall but decrepit old Cypriot gentleman with a long red nose and rheumy eyes who had been rich and influential but had impoverished himself by too much hospitality to women. He was now almost penniless, his politician son paying for his sustenance in this hotel and giving him enough pocket money, *not* to entertain the ladies about us but to go almost nightly to the cinema across the road. When he did not fancy the programme he would sit on the pavement outside the hotel with a group of old cronies who talked, drank coffee and ceaselessly fingered their beads which I presumed to be a kind of rosary used in the Greek Orthodox

Church. I enjoyed talking with the old gentleman who like many elderly *roués* was intelligent and widely read.

The hostess was a truly kind and hospitable old lady who had only a gaunt spinster to help her with all the work of the hotel, but cooked abundant meals at mid-day and at night. Her peasant cookery was not highly varied but her dishes were eatable, or would have been if it were not for the Greek Cypriot insistence on the use of lemons, in soup, with meat and fish and in any other dishes they invented. We ate *dolmas* which in simple terms are vine-leaves stuffed with mince and *keftethes*, meat balls smothered in lemon sauce and pork with quince jam.

The one thing the old lady believed about Englishmen was that they expected immense meals early in the morning. This she must have learned during the British occupation of the island and nothing could convince her to the contrary. As breafast was included in the terms we were paying she made it a point of honour to provide it in alarming quantities. Joseph got off fairly easily being an Indian with exotic tastes, but for me she insisted on quantities of very salt bacon or gristle-and-garlic sausages, or if I was lucky two or three boiled eggs. But her coffee was good and served plentifully in large cups.

The son of the house spoke a little English but disliked the English as he seemed to dislike everyone else. He disapproved of the Greek royal family (not then deposed) the government of Makarios, the demagogue Grivas, the United Nations forces stationed on the island, the Turks, the trades unions which he maintained had ruined his father's business, the Communists and most European peoples. He seemed to make an exception of Joseph and me whom he regarded as lost unfortunates with nowhere to go. There was some competition for his favours among the

women in the hotel but he showed no partiality for any of
them.

He loved one human being, his Mongol younger brother.
The boy was about fourteen years old but his mental age
was of five or six. He had most of the Mongoloid characteristics, grossness, noisiness and restlessness and again like
many of such children he was adored by the members of his
own family who attentively watched his antics and suffered
his raucous voice at all times of the day. No one ever
seemed exasperated by the boy, the other customers treating
him with fondness. He was known to everyone in Limassol
and went about the town moved by curious impulses to
stare, run, or approach strangers; he shouted furiously at
policemen, went to the cinema and ate ice-creams at any
stall he chose without payment. He would march into the
general room at the hotel and his food was always ready for
him, prepared by his mother. When he had received the
plate he would look round the room with little cunning eyes
deciding on the table at which he would sit, choosing one
or another of the customers to watch him eat loudly and
messily. He was very much attached to Joseph who knew
exactly how to humour him gently but managed to keep
him, tactfully, away from me.

If in that hotel there had been a cool bedroom in which I
could work I would have stayed there for a very long time,
for I was never bored and enjoyed the simple events and
conversations of every day.

2

Moreover I was learning a good deal about Cyprus and
the Cypriots. The language was a barrier between them and
me which made me realize what I had lost in leaving the

western Mediterranean where I had been linguistically at home. It was not that the Cypriots did not speak English; most of them did *a little*. That was the point—although any man or woman approached in the street could tell me the way and every shopkeeper or waiter understood what I wanted, there was no one with whom I could really converse as I was used to doing with the English, the French and the Spanish, or Moroccans who spoke one or another of these from birth. This to a man whose trade, and indeed whose life consists of saying exactly what he means and finding out from others without effort what they mean, became tiresome. I found to my surprise that what I remembered of classical Greek or at least the alphabet which was all that my dear father remembered and had taught me unforgettably of the language, enabled me to read and understand posters and public notices and that I could even gather some of the significance of words in a Greek newspaper, but that I could only really converse with Joseph.

This in the end and when I had been in Cyprus for six months or so would be one of the factors in my decision not to make a home here, if I had ever seriously meant to do so. I could never more than remotely belong to a country whose language I did not speak. But at first, in that grubby little hotel, among people incessantly intriguing if a little puzzling to me, I enjoyed myself and came nearer to an understanding of Cypriots than in all the rest of my time on the island. Later, when I had moved to Famagusta which was altogether more of a resort for tourists, I realized that I had come too late to the island. English people spoke of a golden age when the cost of living here was the lowest in Europe, when domestic service was plentiful and willing, when comfortable houses could be bought for £1000 or less and when the privileged car-owner could enjoy the beauty of the countryside without disturbance from revolutionaries or tourists alike. I was not convinced that I should have been so charmed by this reputed paradise, but felt the need of some aspects of it to make the country and the people I met more agreeable. But at Limassol life was different. In uncomfortable cheap quarters and hearing only broken English I felt I was learning each day more about the people of the country and about the home life of the whore than I had ever guessed possible. In other words I was not bored.

I read a little of the long sensational history of Cyprus, periods of bloodshed and of artistic creation, of building and destroying alternately from Neolithic times to the disturbed present. Its successive occupations by Phoenicians, Assyrians, Egyptians, Persians, Romans, Arabs, Venetians Ottoman Turks and British, during most of which there was every kind of warfare, have left its people with no desire for peace. I did not, of course, try to make any detailed study of the history of these wars, but noted with some pleasure that King Richard I of England, Richard Coeur de Lion, hero of every right-minded British schoolboy (at least until his tenth year) married Berengaria of Navarre in Limassol itself.

Of the Turkish population I learned little or nothing while I stayed in that town and so saw only one side of Cypriot life.

But after about a month I had to move, not because of the sordid surroundings but because I could not work. The bedroom was too hot and if I opened the windows, too noisy and it was impossible to write in the restless atmosphere of the general room. I was not impelled by conscience or immediate material necessity to work but because, God help me, I am utterly miserable when I do not do so. Questions about regular hours and inspiration for work about which I wrote in a literary satire called *Wolf From the Door* are meaningless to me. I simply enjoy writing. I have done so since childhood and will continue to do so till my Schaeffer or Parker pen drops from my fingers for the last time.

We made an attempt to find accommodation at a hill-station in the Troödos mountains fifty miles inland, having been told that 'everyone' went there in the summer. The air was crisp and stimulating but the atmosphere, in another sense, was like that of an Anglo-Indian hill-station with a few old British residents left behind here from the days of our rule and although I tried half a dozen hotels, in none of them was there that simple necessity for me, a table on which I could write or one on which Joseph could type.

So when we had returned to the little hotel in Limassol we recognized that there was nothing for it but to move on to Famagusta, the busiest resort and second largest town of Cyprus.

3

Here, I believed, I should find at least some remaining vestiges of that island paradise which had been worth fighting for by so many peoples throughout history, not least of them the British. Salamis, the greatest city of ancient Cyprus was hard by, and although I had yet to learn that Byron's 'sea-born Salamis' referred to the Greek island and not to this no less ancient settlement, I had learned that the scenes in Shakespeare's *Othello*, including the murder scene which I knew by heart were enacted here and that 'the Moor's Tower' was still to be seen. St Barnabas, who though not of the Twelve came to rank as one of the Apostles and took a certainly defined and chronicled part in the earliest years of Christianity, died here less than eighty years after the birth of Christ. Othello's Tower, the famous Sea Gate, was here and also Lala Mustafa, which had once been the cathedral of St Nicholas and by a process in contrast to that of Cordoba Cathedral reverted from the Christian purpose for which it was built to become a great Mosque. There were partly ruined churches built for Nestorians, Armenians, Templars and Hospitallers. I felt sure that there would be enough history in the place to arouse my archaeological interest, which was imaginative rather than scholarly. Somewhere in Famagusta was also the background for the shortest and most festive scene in the works of Shapespeare: 'Othello, Act II. Scene 2, Cyprus. A Street. Enter Othello's Herald with a proclamation; People following. HERALD: It is Othello's pleasure, our noble and valiant general, that, upon certain tidings now arriv'd, importing the mere perdition of the Turkish fleet, every man put himself into triumph; some to dance, some to make bonfires, each man to what sport and revels his addiction leads him; for, besides these beneficial news, it is the celebration of his nuptial. So much was his pleasure should be proclaimed. All offices are open; and there is full liberty of feasting from this present hour of five till the bell have told eleven. Heaven bless the isle of Cyprus and our noble general Othello! Exeunt.'

Almost every race of the ancient world seemed as I read about them to have followed the Herald's orders, so perhaps they would still be doing so, each man enjoying 'what sport and revels his addiction leads him'. Perhaps there would be dance and bonfires as in Othello's day, or their modern counterpart, wild bathing parties on the beach and gay bars. It was all very promising as I was driven there through the seaport of Larnaca which had been the oldest Phoenician settlement in prehistoric Cyprus and had, unless my memory has tricked me, the longest Roman aqueduct I had seen since that of Segovia.

It took me several weeks fully to realize the non-fulfilment of these romantic notions. I had only facetiously supposed that the 'dance and bonfires' were still to be found, but I had imagined a lively and attractive city full of friendly people and classic architecture and if not washed by the foam of the sea from which Aphrodite had risen at least having inviting beaches for the recreation of twentieth century man.

I found—with resentment growing daily—that except for what was known as 'the old city' or 'the Turkish Quarter' Famagusta was a modern watering-place with suburbs of little cramped villas in which soldiers' wives brought up their innumerable progeny, yelling shrill prohibitions to 'put that down', 'come here will you?' and warnings, shouted in the street that conduct would be reported to father when he came home. A major blunder when the modern town had been planned and laid out deprived it of any approach to the sea since ugly blocks of flats had been built almost on the beach and there was no seaside walk, or anything like the conventional promenade of even the meanest European maritime town. To reach the sea itself would-be bathers had to creep down the side passages between apartment blocks or follow for nearly two miles the built-up avenue to find a small area of stony sand from which they could bathe.

The people were resentful. The Greeks abused the Turks whom they employed only in their building projects; the Turks were jealous of the business abilities and possessions of the Greeks, while both hated every kind of foreigner. The Greek-Cypriot business community treated the British with ill-concealed contempt and other Cypriots who did not have to depend on British capital or custom were openly insolent. One or two shopkeepers who had built up a British clientele in the days of our occupation were ingratiating, others patronized all those who did not speak the corrupted local language. This meant in practice that though you could buy without open incivility local wine or highly-priced imported goods, you could not purchase a newspaper or a bottle of ink, articles which produced no considerable profit, without feeling that you were receiving a favour. Even British banks, manned by half-educated Greeks, were not only inefficient but lacking in ordinary politeness and in cafés, restaurants and hotels you could only obtain civility by over-paying for it.

With this went a peculiar form of pretentiousness and financial snobbery. Everybody was out to keep up with the Joneses and what made this notable was that the Joneses did not exist. The Sunday *paseo* familiar in every Spanish town when families dress up and walk through a street or park to criticize one another, was on a grander scale, a *paseo* by motor-car. Each Sunday from about ten o'clock in the morning till two o'clock in the afternoon when the residents presumably went to their homes for lunch, they drove round Famagusta by a specified route, each car polished to brilliance, every family occupying all the seats. It was not a gay or a lively occasion, the pace was slow and the faces seen through the car windows were rigid and serious, but everyone who owned a car, which meant almost the entire population of the town joined in it, or was considered a pauper and an outcast who did not know what was due to his fellow townsmen.

There were so-called supermarkets where English products cost far more than in their country of origin and were limited to those standard goods which are supplied to us everywhere abroad in the seeming belief that we want nothing else—mass-produced jam, breakfast cereals, butter and margarine proudly claiming to be indistinguishable from one another in taste, manufactured salad cream, meat paste made from cereals faintly flavoured and coloured with some meaty extract, processed cheese, unanalysable cooking fat, bottles of sugary syrup passing as lemonade, tinned fish and various forms of a substance sold as 'pork loaf'.

There was the town market where almost the only products sold were citrus fruits. If the meat was locally produced it had a leatheriness and stringiness surpassing that of Spain (which is saying a lot), and if imported all the taste had been frozen out of it. There was no fish beyond the occasional squid, 'white fish' presumably being sold to the Services stationed round the town, and very few vegetables. These were the only provisions for the (chiefly) British tourists of whom there were a few remaining in the town from the summer now past.

Above all, it was an unhappy city. The Cypriots never seemed to laugh—perhaps they were too busy counting the sudden gains which had come to them in recent years—and everyone seemed to grudge the very air of their island to foreigners. I wished I had never left Limassol. Sleazy and uncomfortable, it yet showed a kind of friendliness which the prosperous bourgeoisie of Famagusta denied us.

4

Before resigning myself to living in Famagusta I went to look round the capital, Nicosia, and to visit Kyrenia across the island which was reputed to be a sure refuge and delight. Nicosia had a trying climate, as hot as Bombay in the summer and cut by chilly winds in the winter. It had, however, a reasonably good hotel where we lunched well and were civilly served. Joseph needed to renew his passport and was amused to note that although India had no consular facilities in all Cyprus and had to refer her citizens to the nearest office in Beirut, the General just appointed to command all the United Nations troops in the island was Indian, a pleasant youngish man whom we met in the hotel restaurant. Nicosia would have been all very well for a fortnight's stay if one were a Greek-speaking millionaire, but it had little to offer to me.

Kyrenia was sad and funny. Four years after that visit I saw a memorable television programme depicting a colony of mummified Britons left behind after Indian independence in Ootacumund, organizing a hyena hunt (the fox being unknown) with a Sikh as MFH, defiantly frequenting a deserted British Club, holding flower-shows and bazaars directed by a masterly Memsahib who talked of 'the natives' and generally keeping alive the manners of another age. Kyrenia was not quite such an anachronism but the English people, relics of a happier time for their kind, obstinately clung to the illusion that Kyrenia was not a mixture of a Greek Tunbridge Wells and a resort of mixed climate on the Costa del Sol. They chatted in the English-owned bars at night oblivious of the world, even of the island, which surrounded them.

So in order to work I had to find a home in Famagusta, and this I did easily enough *at a price*. Four years ago the western world had not been totally abandoned to the property speculator so that I was surprised to find only one kind of dwelling-place in all that city, the so-called furnished holiday flat, a couple of rooms, bathroom and kitchen into which skeleton necessities had been dumped to be let at a minimum of £20 a week, not per flat but per occupant. The property firms of Cyprus had been more intelligent than most of those in Las Palmas and did not let their flats to parties who could divide the expenses among themselves and so have a reasonably-priced holiday. What money there was to be made they wanted and so let their premises at so much a head, knowing that even these would cost less than hotel accommodation, the only alternative. In England the property speculators learned the same methods but did not use the same wording so that although a flat large enough for three costs three times as much as a single flat, the rent was not admitted to be per head.

Otherwise there was nothing to be done unless anyone was so much in love with Famagusta that he was prepared to risk buying an exorbitantly priced home there, taking the risk of all the chances and grim possibilities that beset the island. I could not, and had no inclination to do anything of the sort, so I began to look for a furnished flat for the winter.

Then befell one of those things which, I must gladly admit, happened on a number of occasions in Cyprus and assured me that I had misjudged these strange people, full of mixed blood and surprises.

I called on, fruitlessly, a number of agents and landlords who all prospered by exactly the same methods, that was by advertising in London newspapers a cosy flat 'with service' and all found, and on the strength of this filling the scores of flats they owned all through the summer with families looking for sunlight. Some of these flats were miles from the sea, some of them lost in streets of dreary little houses and all of them were barely furnished from a central pool of wretched tables, chairs and beds which they put into each flat as they were required. The occupants soon learned, after they had arrived and taken up residence in the flats for which they had paid in advance that complaints would be received with smiles and promises, but that nothing would be done, and so spent their holidays no more fruitfully than their compatriots on the coasts of Spain or in Malta and returned to England deciding whether they would speak of a hateful or of a lovely holiday, according to whether they wanted envy or sympathy from their neighbours.

But a miracle happened to me. I went to a firm whose reputation was rather better than most and saw one of two brothers named Constantinou who owned it, and before I had finished explaining what I wanted and how impossible it seemed to find it, I realized that I had caught the sympathy of this very hard-headed man who had never (I was told later) been known to budge an inch or show any understanding of the needs of anyone who did business with him. He questioned me closely about my work and understood that I needed a table large enough to write on and enough heat in the room to enable me to sit there for long periods.

'A writer,' he mused, 'I don't think we've ever had a writer here before.'

It seemed, it seems today, quite impossible that this commercially-minded married man of thirty-five with growing children and an obsession with the stock market should give the least importance to the fact that I wrote books and I made no pretence of being deeply interested in his country or anxious to see all its wonders. I can only say that he took up the matter of my stay as though it was a personal responsibility and persuaded the brother who was his partner to do the same. He let me one of his flats in a good position at a rent of about half of what he usually received for it, even in winter, and furnished it with the best of his stock. He provided an electric heater and other things not contracted for in the lease and brought to the flat many

small domestic necessities. Also he found for us a 'daily' of
sorts and thereafter once a week at least he would call to see
whether there was anything else we needed and he never
forgot to enquire after the progress of my book. I call this a
miracle and I think that to those who know the character of
the Greek Cypriots, born under a foreign yoke and brought
up to fight for themselves against almost everyone and
everything in the world, it will seem no less.

The flat was one of a pair on the first floor of a house in a
street leading up from the beach about two miles from the
centre of Famagusta. This meant that I could walk down to
the water's edge in a few moments as I had never been able
to do in Dieppe, Las Palmas, Gibraltar or Limassol from
which I had come. I have always been able to think creatively
when I hear the sound of waves breaking near me as I did in
my teens when I would watch the sun setting over the sea
from the 'promenades' of seaside towns and be stirred to
emotion by the sight. Facing South here I saw that sun rise
over the Mediterranean but only its reflection on the water
in the evening. But I worked then harder than I had done
since my Tangerine years, completing a novel called *Under
the Rose Garden* which unaccountably disturbed me as I
wrote it.

5

For a month or more I was satisfied to remain in that
suburb, working and occasionally going to the local *bistro*
where the proprietor, a stocky Greek Cypriot who had
owned a small restaurant in London for many years and
spoke in the manner of a Soho cockney, could produce a
meal of sorts and gave us oddments of local information.
He made a complicated arrangement with a taxi-driver who

took us to the town centre once or twice a week, and introduced us to the weight-lifter son of one of the market stall-holders from whom we bought vegetables and who led us round the other stalls trying to find fish or edible meat.

In front of that small cafe-restaurant was a space open to the sea, the first break in the buildings along the shore from the city. Here open army trucks would pull up on most days carrying United Nations troops, chiefly British and Scandinavian, for a swim in the sea which they enjoyed noisily. Except when they came the seashore was deserted but for an occasional serious and solitary young man who mooned along much as I did, never bringing a girl with him since customs and taboos about courtship in Cyprus forbade not only public dalliance but even 'going out' together by young couples.

But as time passed I did not feel deserted or bored in or around that temporary home. I was realizing that Cyprus was not the country for me but pale sunshine continued throughout the early winter and small things amused me and Joseph, like the ear-splitting yells of the old lady who lived below and was paid to pump water to our tank on the roof. She spoke no language known to us but this did not prevent her from rousing the street when she wanted to talk at length with her neighbours four doors away. There was also an old character who dressed up in national costume to sell to the British holiday-makers and inhabitants vegetables and eggs at prices far higher than those in the market, but gave his customers (as the *bistro*-proprietor explained to us) a touch of local colour which they believed authentic and recorded with their cameras.

The flat next door to ours was taken by two middle-aged English sisters, almost too perfect in character, enthusiastic Anglicans and church workers from somewhere in the

Home Counties, speaking of relatives who belonged to one or another of the professions and worried about leaving their garden at home. It was the first time, they said, that they had been away for Christmas and it was only because one of them suffered from asthma that they had ventured abroad. They did not much care for television but, anxious to show their broad-mindedness, sat through an innocuous programme. They also made English scones, since they said nothing of the sort could be obtained in the shops and invited us to tea in order to enjoy them hot, which we did. They found Cyprus salubrious but were homesick for their English parish. Very occasionally they succumbed to a glass of sweet sherry but said no to whisky and were quite distressed at the mention of gin. They were dears and put greeting cards under our door when Christmas came.

Their scorn for local television programmes would not have been surprising even if at home they had been enthusiastic viewers. I was yet to realize, as I came to do in the following years, that television in England is not only by far the best in Europe (and I have viewed for considerable periods in German, French, Spanish and Italian), but the only system really worth watching at all. The various sub-stations in places like Gibraltar and Cyprus which exist by putting out potted programmes imported cheaply from the United States and Australia, only irritate and reproach one for time-wasting. In Cyprus sometimes there were local programmes, stories of intrigues among peasants in the villages, while on one evening a week the programmes were Turkish. Otherwise we had Cilla Black in weekly doses or the interminable banalities of *Peyton Place* which were then about 'to cease upon the midnight with no pain' to me, or I imagine, to anyone else. But we saw some good films in one of the five thriving cinemas in the town and I had my daily

diversion of *The Times* crossword (of which Compton
Mackenzie once said to me that the hardest moment of his
day was when he had to put it down and commence work).
There was also a sham British pub in the town where
soldiers from the nearby base drank imported light ale sold
by a Greek barman.

It was here I met a young English corporal who made me
feel old, not because of the difference in our ages but
because he demonstrated how 'the Army had changed since
my day', a sentiment frequent among the old codgers of
fiction. He spoke precisely in a semi-cultivated provincial
manner and was doing some technical work which we
should have dismissed under the name of 'Signals'. He was
earning a thousand or two pounds a year 'all found', with
free transport for frequent holidays at home. He came to
visit my flat and confessed that he did not read anything
except books on his own subject, but when he heard that I
was a writer wanted a copy of one of my books 'to take home
on leave', if I would write and sign a dedication in it. He
would even, he said munificently, be prepared to pay for it,
but disliking the sentiment of this I refused. He had
brought his wife out and secured married quarters for the
two of them, 'quite a decent little flat with three rooms,' but
she was now living with another fellow who kept his
quarters and her. 'Quite usual' he assured me, but when he
had left the flat I thought impotently *eheu fergaces*, *Postume*,
Postume, *labuntur anni*, and remembered the days when

There was two-an'-thirty Sergeants,
There was Corp'rals forty-one,
There was just nine 'undred rank an' file
To swear to a touch o' the sun

and swear obscenely with lusty blasphemy when we
sweated together thirty years ago and played ha'penny nap

because we had no more than a few rupees with which to gamble.

Another anomalous visitor to the flat was a Cypriot lady who had been recommended to us and whom we had engaged at considerable expense as a 'char', but who expected to share not only our meals but our beds, an elegant and flirtatious young woman who arrived by car and had never heard of housework. It took us some days to convince her that we only wanted the washing-up and cleaning done but when this dawned on her she drove away sulkily and we never saw her again except when she came to claim money in lieu of the notice she had not given us.

However, consultation with the restaurant-keeper brought us a podgy little mother of a family who came to the house every afternoon smiling but silent (since she spoke no English), and worked in a businesslike way, hanging our washing on the roof. She had worked for an English family, we learned, and reminded me of the attitudes of an earlier age—not feudal but of middle-class British superiority to foreigners of all sorts, the age when Cyprus had been a sunlit place of retirement for Britons who had completed their life's work in India or Africa and feared their own climate too much to settle at home in their old age.

There were other reminders of that era in Famagusta, pieces of Victorian furniture which had been sold and left behind by the departing English, sports and sports clubs with English names, London banks, British clothes and the language itself which was commonly spoken, or at any rate understood, by most educated Cypriots. To my astonishment there was also, rather pathetically, a British Club. In one room of an old double-fronted house to which I was taken one morning half a dozen Britons met with something of an air of defiance, and exchanged family gossip while they drank beer. It was evidently a daily gathering at which news was exchanged of events of interest to this mini-community, relic of a more formidable organization in times past.

I was asked with notable casualness about my war-service by the Secretary, who was seemingly considering me as a candidate for membership. When I said that I had been commissioned in the Gurkhas I was a made man, but abandoned a moment later when in answer to a question of whether I lived alone, I said no, I lived with my Indian secretary.

January passed and still there was pale sunlight and still I knew no more of the old city of Famagusta than I had learned from the occasional guide book. Now and again I noticed the heavily guarded Land Gate to the Turkish Quarter in which were the chief antiquities of the place, where taxis or residents in the modern city were discouraged or forbidden to enter. Behind that gate, I argued, were wonders and delights which I only imagined, meanwhile promising myself that the right time to pass through the gate and make discoveries would come when I had worked enough to justify a sightseeing holiday and rest. Reports about the Cypriot Turks ('Anatolian peasants' wrote Patrick Kinross who knows the race) were common in Varosha, the newer part of the city in which I lived, and I heard many reports about the antiquities there and in Salamis beyond, but I waited until the Spring.

6

Then I went into 'the Turkish Quarter', the real city of Famagusta and found that though its beauties and points of

D

interest were all that I had hoped, here too was that over-
lying sense of sadness, almost of despair, which I had found
in all Cyprus, a scarcely definable atmosphere which may
have been partly created in my own mind by my own
foreignness to everything Greek or Turkish. Few people
smiled and nobody laughed outright and looking back on
those six months on the island I cannot remember anyone
showing real pleasure in anything. The so-called places of
amusement were noisy enough but the customers were
glum and watchful rather than gay while they went about
their enjoyment with a solemnity that oppressed one. The
one quality, I decided when I had come to know the Turks,
which they had in common with the Greeks was that they
had little sense of humour and no gaiety.

They were also to me the most completely *foreign* people
I had met. Perhaps because they were Muslims like the
Moroccans among whom I had lived for so long, I expected
that they would have some resemblances in character with
them though I had been warned that I would not find this.
It was almost shocking to find that two races which
followed Islam and were alike in the colour of their skin had
nothing, but *nothing* else in common. It was painful to find
myself so entirely without knowledge or understanding of
any people and to know that it was too late now to learn. I
saw that they were as surly and resentful as the Greeks, but
I was prepared to understand and sympathize with this. I
had even contemplated smashing all precedents by looking
for a home in the old city. What I found hard to bear was
their entire blank indifference, not merely to me a foreigner,
but to their own fate or their own surroundings. There was
in their faces no suggestion of pride, or joy, or ambition—
only lassitude and dull satiety.

The first place I went to just after entering the city was an

open-air restaurant with a reputation for the excellence of
its *mezes*, these being a collection of hot foods, meat,
chicken, fish, vegetables, artfully produced on separate
small dishes which usually make up a whole meal as
smalbröd often does in Scandinavian countries. I had eaten
mezes with greater or less satisfaction elsewhere in Cyprus
but heard from a polite if unanimated waiter that we were
too late that evening to be served.

We went on next day to see a large mosque which like
others I have seen in India and South Africa seemed very
impressive but left no impression in the mind after I had
visited it. We climbed to the heights of the Citadel and saw
the open space beneath Othello's Tower where the play had
been produced in recent years. We went on to Salamis and
spent a day among its (chiefly) Roman remains and as we
returned through the city of Famagusta were offered some
pieces of Mycenaean pottery by a Turkish shopkeeper.

There is a large under-the-counter trade in this in all
Turkish sections of Cyprus towns since the Government,
regarded by the Turks as Greek and alien, has forbidden
their export in an effort to prevent Cypriot antiquities from
turning up everywhere in the antique market as they do
today. This gives the Turks who are indifferent to such
things, an opportunity to sell bowls, aryballos, amphorae
and the rest to tourists who secrete them in their luggage
when they leave Cypriot ports. I did not know of these
regulations at the time so I cannot say how I should have
faced the nice points of conscience involved, but bargained
and bought from an open stall.

Then, back from days among the ancient ruins of
Salamis and Famagusta, I began to look for a means of
escaping from the island to find another refuge. The dull
sadness of the place, unbroken by laughter or song (except

the moaning Cypriot melodies of the country people played on unfamiliar instruments), had begun to oppress me and I saw that the impregnable strangeness of everything Cypriot, alien in a basic sense not only to me but to all the peoples I had known, would never be broken down. Perhaps if I had come here to live in my receptive youth I might have understood and liked these people but not on finding them first at my present age. I must return to the Western Mediterranean or even nearer home.

When I went to a travel agency I found in charge of it a friendly Englishman named Ronald Bradbury who had married a Parsee girl and the two became our friends. Frany Bradbury delighted in entertaining us to large lovely Indian meals which she cooked supremely well. She had the amiable custom of preparing about twice the quantity that the four of us could possibly eat and packing half of it in plastic containers, like a take-away oriental restaurant in England today, to present to us when we departed. This made us almost sorry to leave Cyprus but her husband had already arranged passages for us on a steamer bound for Naples, from where we were to go to Rome and eventually to Tunis, in which city we had decided to settle. So we set out on the next stage of our journey.

Five

Tunis

When I began to write this series of books my intention was that they should describe the world about me during a lifetime which I hoped would stretch through most of this century, the people, places, sights, sounds and tastes I had observed, with something of the achievements and failures of a literary jack-of-all-trades who had experienced much and had a keen memory for detail, but that I should not indulge in personal introspection and should avoid those confessions about sex and religion which seemed to obsess many autobiographers. My subject was the sensual world, not the intimate life of the author. I do not now intend to depart from that plan but over religion I feel I must make some explanations both for the reader and for me, since only by formulating them in my mind and setting them down can I begin to understand them. From Cyprus I went with Joseph to Rome where we were received in audience—along with many more—by the Pope, and I want to know and to try to say exactly what that meant to me.

I have told in *The Altar in the Loft* how in my thirteenth year I wanted to become a Catholic and how my Protestant mother resolved that I should do nothing of the sort, and how my father who knew nothing of such things loyally supported her. 'Your mother knows all about that, my boy. You must do what she tells you.' An unhappy rift with my parents ensued ending in a pact between my father and me by which I was allowed to go to Mass if I would promise not to be Received till I came of age. I have told in *The Glittering Pastures* how on my twenty-first birthday in the parish church of San Isidro near Buenos Aires I was conditionally baptized and although I have always maintained that I am to all intents a born Catholic, having been throughout my whole intelligent life a member of the Church, it was from that day, June 20 1924, that I actually became one.

But the fervour which had helped me to struggle with my parents evaporated with the years and became little more than a worldly man's temporal allegiance to the Church. I entered my name as 'RC' when I joined the Army and went to Mass once or twice a year without giving much thought to the matter. I felt something like detestation, learned in my years of instruction, for those who claimed to be Catholics though they 'disagreed' with the Church on particular doctrines, like Eternal Damnation and the Immaculate Conception. I would be all or nothing, I decided, accept the whole faith or dispute it utterly, and although I could never make up my mind to do either of these with finality this ambivalence meant in practical terms that I became, I suppose, a 'lapsed Catholic'.

There were times when I was forced towards some kind of conclusion. During a lull in the only battle I have been in, that for Diego Suarez in 1942, the Catholic chaplain to the

Force, Father McDonnell, told me that he was about to say Mass for Brigadier Festing (afterwards Field Marshal Sir Francis Festing, GCB, CB, KBE, DSO, DL) and that he could give me Conditional Absolution if I wished to receive Communion. I had not taken any of the Sacraments for years and felt that it would be a kind of cowardice to do so in that moment of stress, so I puzzled good Father McDonnell by refusing.

Another puzzlement arose when Joseph came to work for me with a Faith inherited from ancestors converted by St Francis Xavier, like that of most South Indian Christians. He naturally expected more from me than occasional attendance at Mass but throughout the thirty years he has been with me the anomalous situation went on. It made division and chaos in my mind now that we were, in the literal sense, going to Rome.

It has never been resolved. There must be devout and faithful Christians who will understand, however impatient it may make them, the difficulties of this shilly-shallying and sentimentality, as they will see it. I can only say that I am devoted to my religion even if I can't believe in it (or all of it, which is the same thing), that I still proudly call myself a Catholic, that I have prayed for faith to a God in whom I cannot altogether believe, and that in the meanwhile, however illogically, no one is more indignant than I at the so-called reforms in the Church, the loss of Latin Mass (which is nowadays said not only in secular languages but by a priest standing with his back to the East), at concessions to so-called 'progressive' theologians and at all the fratting with Protestants on a doctrinal level which Catholics are allowed and even encouraged to do by the Church whose uncompromising doctrines I accepted at such cost to myself as a young boy. I watched a Midnight

Mass on Television this Christmas which might have been a commercial advertizing a manufactured religion rather than an act of devotion. It was something between a parade of the Sally Army with waltz-time hymns instead of a liturgy, or an evening concert by Jess Yates and his boys, and bore little or no relationship with the Mass as I knew it.

However Rome itself had no disappointments for me in that Spring of 1970, and certainly none for Joseph whose first visit to the Holy City this was. We disembarked in Naples for the third visit in my lifetime to that enchanted city but had no time to do more than walk through the Galeria in which I had found adventure more than forty years earlier.

It was warm and sunny in Rome and I looked for that hotel near the Borghese gardens in which in 1938 I had been awakened in the small hours by the nightingales. I had forgotten the name (the Flora, I think), and put up at another hotel nearby, but the nightingales could be heard no more, only the restless din of traffic.

That visit to Rome was in a particular sense for Joseph's sake, not only because here was the only Indian Embassy on our route towards Tunis and he needed a new passport and a visa to enter Tunisia, but for more cogent reasons. When almost thirty years before he had become for me an adopted son and left the parents and family he loved to follow me to Europe, I had resolved to take him to Rome, to see St Peter's and have an audience with the Pope, as every one of the thirty million Indian Christians longed to do with a fervour that matched the Mohammedans' ambition to go to Mecca. This was the first opportunity for it, so it meant a fulfilment for me as well as for him.

I decided not to attempt to show him everything in Rome in the ten days' time we had, much of which would be

taken up with waiting at the Indian and Tunisian consulates.
I knew that once a week the Pope was 'at home' in St
Peter's to anyone who wanted to call on him there, and that
on Sunday mornings he appeared at a window in the
Vatican to bless those in the square below. We were present
on both occasions, struggling up the crowded steps of the
Cathedral as millions before us have done to wait for the
frail but vital-looking old Prelate to be carried in, and we
heard him talk to us and other British pilgrims in English.
It was surprising to me, as I had found it on previous
occasions, that such a vast congregation should need so
little guidance or supervision from the Swiss Guards and
Cathedral staff—only an occasional camera click disturbing
the tense hush about us, till the outbreaks of hand-clapping
came suddenly and surprisingly from the enormous mass of
the faithful and curious alike. They gave the Pope a reception as prolonged and fervent as that accorded to a television
artist by an invited audience but a hundred times magnified
under the far-away dome of the great basilica.

What is it that motivates, that inspires this great multi-
tude, gathering from all over the world to greet one man?
Sheer religious fervour? Pride or a kind of patriotism?
Inspired hysteria? Ardour of self-dedication to God and
His spokesman? The need of men for someone greater and
better than themselves which once made them cry for a king
to rule over them? Or the flippant delight in a visit to the
Pope which made Wilde write 'my position is curious: I am
not a Catholic: I am simply a violent Papist'? Whatever its
nature it was felt by both of us and remains vivid in my
mind. Joseph wrote to his father and mother, then in their
late eighties, and to his two brothers and sister to describe
the occasion though I noticed that after three decades of
speaking English, he no longer used the complicated

twirling Tamil script in which he had written home when he first came to England.

2

The Colosseum had changed, not of course in actual appearance, but in my mind when I visited it. Since Mussolini had restored parts of it, regarding the great arena as his own private playground, very little had been done. Of the time when I had sat alone on the stone seats on my visit before the war I wrote: 'It took no feat of clairvoyance to see that vast amphitheatre populated with a Roman crowd. One could call them up as easily as a Hollywood producer with a generous budget and hear them cheering the lions. But I reached the Colosseum in the late afternoon when none but a few stray sightseers were left and there was an uncanny silence in the place which played on the imagination. There were no pale and ancient ghosts here, tired by the centuries, but swarthy and vivacious phantoms with the cruel savage stares of wild animals.' Now it was no more than a huge ancient construction built to hold fifty thousand people, magnificent and impressive but no longer haunted. I heard no more in imagination of the lions' roar or the gladiators' death-cries and saw no toga-draped figures climbing the stairs. The change was in me, from the young man who called up ghosts in any place heavy with history, to the more realistic middle-aged traveller who wondered where the nearest restaurant was to be found.

Nor did the Catacombs stir anew my sensibilities. I was surprised to find how much I remembered of them from that time when I had been led through them a quarter of a century ago. Joseph was awed and interested but more by their part in early eccesiastical history than in the atmos-

phere which had once cast a spell over me. Ours is a prosaic
age and I have never been much attracted by what are
miscalled 'psychic phenomena'.

All the other monuments and marvels of Rome remain
still unexamined by me, though periodically I dream, as I
do of Athens, that one day I will give myself a month with
nothing to do but go sightseeing there, knowing that it will
never happen. Nor am I enough of a devoted antiquarian
to make the most of that month, even if it were possible.
And lately—shameful confession—I am more than half
reconciled to seeing ancient places on television. I do not
suppose that film and commentary about one of the beautiful
relics of the human past like the Alhambra, the Colossus of
Rhodes or the city of Fatehpur Sikri do more than tease the
imagination, but I realize that most probably these are all I
shall have time for.

The journey back to Naples was uneventful and we went
on board a packet boat bound for Tunis. We passed Capri
at night as I had done once before, suitably soliloquizing
that though San Michele is an empty memorial to the
garrulous old gentlemen who owned it, there must still be
traces of that lost world described by Norman Douglas and
Roger Peyrefitte, the little world of Count d'Adelsward
Fersen and Nino Cesarini, of the Café Morgano and the
Hotel Quisisana, of Ephy Lovatelli and the Misses Wolcott-
Perry, and the rest of that exotic company whose adventures,
under the names chosen for them by several novelists, I had
followed, but nowhere more hilariously or affectionately
than in Compton Mackenzie's nostalgic masterpiece *Vestal
Fire*. I woke the next morning to find that the ship was in
the docks at Palermo besieged by a hundred or two Tunisians wanting to return to their home after working in Europe
or going on a shopping spree in Sicily.

Then, late in the evening we reached La Golette, the port
of Tunis, and realized that the city itself was two miles
inland. The only form of conveyance available was provided by mini-cabs and we had to take two of these to carry
us and our luggage to the hotel in which we had booked
rooms. It was altogether an inauspicious entry to the
country, a long wait in draughty Customs sheds then a drive
in darkness across the marshy flats to the main street and a
dispute about whether our baggage should be carried into
the hotel by street loafers, the taximen who had brought us,
or the hotel staff. It was almost midnight before we could
settle down for a drink in the hotel's cubby hole of a bar,
served by a tall Tunisian negro.

3

From the first weeks in Tunis I decided to make it my
home. Whether or not I said or wrote that I expected to
remain for the rest of my life I do not remember, but I
certainly thought so. Instead of looking about me critically
and noting this or that advantage in the place or wondering
whether the drawbacks would drive me away, I viewed it,
with all its attractions and faults as my home and expressed
this by sending for my furniture and books from Tangier,
though the only route they could take was by ship via
Marseilles.

Within a fortnight I had found a flat which seemed to
promise permanence. It was in one of the central streets of the
city, which like that of my home in Tangier was called after
a writer. There I had lived in Rue Samuel Pepys; here, more
exotically, my street perpetuated the name of Ibn Khaldoun
the Arabic historian of the fourteenth century. It was on the
first floor and had a room twenty-five feet long with three

tall windows looking on the street, a room whose large proportions were not matched in the smaller rooms to the rear of the building but which in itself gave me scope for endless planning even before my furniture arrived.

I soon realized that in coming to Tunis, modern and architecturally uninteresting though the city itself was, I was able with an effort of the imagination to return in mind to the punic world of Flaubert's *Salammbô*, that huge blown-up bloodthirsty novel of which most of the action passed in Carthage or in the country round. Between Tunis and the sea-shore the miles of marshy lakeland were haunted by pink flamingoes. From the city to the seaside suburbs and to the remains of Carthaginian ruins ran a railway line with stations named Salammbô, Amilcar, Carthage and the rest, while among the stony sand-dunes could still be seen the outlines of the streets and temples of the city. No one seemed to think it noteworthy that one could take railway tickets to these stations and step out of the train on roads made long before the Romans came, where Astarte, goddess of the moon and protectress of Carthage, whom Virgil called Queen Dido, built her funeral pyre and destroyed herself for the love of Aeneas. No one but an archaeologist troubled to remember that here the Carthaginians raised money to support the glorious armies of Hannibal, or that here the terrible goddess Tanit demanded the sacrifice of thousands of little children burnt alive for her dishonour. Rows of seaside villas have risen tidily over the ruins of Carthage.

But the city of Tunis, a mixture of French, Italian and Berber traditions, with only a touch of British left by the events of the last war, was insistently and raucously about us. The flat I took belonged to an Italian woman and several of the flats above it were rented to Italian and French families. The Tunisian restaurant in which we ate daily while we were waiting for the arrival of furniture had been owned by a French proprietor and retained a little of French tradition debased to North African standards, while the people seen in the streets were Berbers, who like other Maghrebis, call themselves Arabs, or less pretentiously Tunisians, Algerians and Moroccans respectively.

The city was cut by the wide rather fine central highway, the Avenue Bourguiba which ran between the main shops and offices and cathedral to the ancient gateway of Bab Bhar which marked the entrance to the *medina* of narrow streets and the little shops and stalls of Tunisians, Indians and Jews. It was all on a much more imposing scale than Tangier, for Tunis is essentially a capital city with embassies and European quarters. There were few tourists, for visitors who arrived by air or sea stayed only an hour or two in Tunis before making for resorts farther South, Gabes and the oases, Monastir, Sfax, Mahdia or the holiday island of Gharbi.

But Tunis had its own fascinations. The Avenue Bourguiba was built like the Ramblas in Barcelona, a wide tree-shaded promenade down its centre, and two roads of one-way traffic running on each side of it, a lay-out particularly promising for a connoisseur of city populations like myself. For me and for Joseph it might almost be said that the town revolved round the Café de Paris, the immense meeting-place about halfway up the street, where tables were crowded with an ever-changing populace in the café itself and along its pavements. Here if anywhere I realized what the Parisians mean by the 'café life' which so many of them in one sense or another enjoy. To have a place to which one can go almost nightly, to be recognized by various groups, talk and pass time, eat if one wants but above all drink as little or as much as one wishes while the hours of a long evening pass in gossip and good-feeling, meant a great deal to us and was a distinct factor in deciding us to settle in Tunis. There were aspects of the city which later I came to detest, but even as I recall it today the Café de Paris joins in my mind those few places of entertainment in various cities of the world in which I should like to wake from sleep—Purohit's in Bombay, the Parade Bar in Tangier, the Alte Herrlichkeit in Monschau, Chez Francois in Diego Suarez, the Bell Inn at Smarden, the Oro del Rhin in Barcelona or the Richmond in Buenos Aires. In all of them I have found interest and happiness out of all proportion to the buildings themselves or the drinks served in them, in all of them I have made friends and done what business-men would call 'wasted time'.

There were other attractions in Tunis. On the little railway, whose trains had the habit, pleasant or alarming according to one's degree of agility, of stopping only a moment or two at stations and hurriedly pulling out without warning, one could go out to the beaches with very little delay or expense and lie in the sun or swim with the graceful youth of Tunisia around one, till nightfall came suddenly and early. One could eat—though not luxuriously—at little restaurants all along that coast to the small spectacular hilltop town of Sidi-Bou-Said, where there were hotels and cafés and a *souk* selling Tunisian handycrafts.

The British Embassy in Tunis had been entered by a hostile mob inflamed by false propaganda during the Six-Day Arab-Israeli War, but it had been lavishly refurnished in apology by the Tunisian Government and here I found, in charge of the British Council, an Englishman with whom, and his family, I made friends at once, the only compatriots except the teetotaller Ambassador and the kind and friendly Consul I knew during my year's stay in the country. Tom and Kit Morray and their children were friends indeed and remain so today and it was delightful to find in such a markedly foreign city people who came not only from my own country but my own tradition and also from my own county of Kent. I had long since outlived the feeble snobbery of wanting to avoid one's countrymen abroad as I had outlived dependence on them, or the need to spend time amongst them, but finding this family was like meeting forgotten cousins in a strange place.

The Ambassador was a Scot who had Oxford Group (or is it Moral Disarmament?) tendencies which were embarrassing to us all, particularly when he offered nothing but mineral water to thirsty Tunisians who expected to toast the Queen of England on her birthday in something more appropriate. He was a good conscientious fellow in other ways and I found him friendly to both me and Joseph. But more amicable to us both—to me somewhat unexpectedly— was the Indian Chargé d'Affaires, Krishna Bindra, one of the first officials of either my own or Joseph's country who has accepted us and our relationship with obvious pleasure. He did not think it in any way remarkable that I who had known his country as a soldier during the war had adopted Joseph as a son and had exploited his talents as a secretary for nearly thirty years. We went to his house for delicious Indian meals on a number of occasions and met members of his staff and other Indian friends.

Among these was Prem Baharani, member of a Sindhi-Hindu family which had settled in Tunis before my lifetime. I have known people of his race and religion in many countries, in Pakistan itself, in Bombay and right across the world wherever their tribal trading posts with the West flourish. These consist of shops where Indian and Japanese articles are sold, everything from Benares brass to Japanese cigarette lighters and cameras, Indian mock ivory and scent,

with manufactured toys from Hong Kong. You see these
little shops in the Atlantic and Mediterranean islands, in
Muslim countries and Christian capitals. Their owners are
deeply religious, indefatigably industrious and by their own
standards strictly honourable. They make their morning
devotions before the safe and work at their books scrupulously and late at night. Like the Jews they keep their
national conscience and like to stand well in the opinion of
their own people among whom communication is close
from Bombay to Buenos Aires and back. They are bound
together by ties of marriage and commerce, and are keen if
inscrutable psychologists trusting their own judgments so
implicitly that they will capitalize another man on his say-so
without a signature if they think he is credit-worthy and
they are very rarely disillusioned.

Of this remarkable race my friend Prem Baharani was a
scion but he had also some qualities which I like to think
Western, a carefree generosity and humour which made him
less clannish and narrow than most of his people. Like the
Chargé d'Affaires he was one of the few men of either
Joseph's race or mine who have entirely understood and
approved of our relationship.

Beyond these people our only friends were Tunisians
during the whole year we remained in that country. There
were no more than a score of English people in the capital,
as we found when we had to obtain Residence Permits. I
was, in fact, the only Englishman in Tunis who came there
for no purpose but to live without involvement in the
Embassy or British education or commerce.

4

As in the whole Muslim world, it was the men in Tunis
who worked to gain a living while the women kept the

house and brought up the children, but occidentals should not fall into the error of supposing that by this the women lack authority in the family. They possess a sovereignty which would make the most articulate members of Women's Lib hysterical with envy and it is the matriarch who rules the tribe. The men are not only the breadwinners; they are the playboys, gamblers, chatterers and revellers too, so that strangers who do not know these people and see only men in places of amusement get a totally false impression of the status of women. Even in Tunis, an up-to-date city as they go in the Arab world, one rarely saw in the Café de Paris, for instance, a Tunisian woman, even when there were European girls in plenty. But this made the men more companionable and genial, more receptive to strangers, good fellows and good fun. In the cafés, restaurants, *hammams*, sport centres, night-clubs and brothels the young and old men of Tunis enjoyed themselves without the company of their own women—an all-male society so far as appearances went. I felt amost as I had done in the Army, and Joseph filled the flat with young friends among whom he was notably popular and at home. While the Tunisians, as hospitable as all the people of North Africa when they have accepted a foreigner, would ask him to their homes for huge meals of *cous-cous* or *tajines*. He learned to speak French sufficiently in a matter of months and went to French films several evenings a week. It was the time when Alain Delon seemed to dominate the French commercial cinema and in the many Tunisian cinés, the films, particularly French or French-dubbed and American, were always up-to-date. There were also Indian films which, all over the Maghreb, are more popular than the gaudy Arabic-speaking films from Egypt.

So from one week to another I scarcely spoke English.

With Joseph I had the kind of communication that exists between two people who have lived for many years under the same roof working and entertaining others but not feeling the necessity to talk merely for the sake of politeness. In the thirty years of our association, I realize as I write this, we have never said good-morning to one another and we exchanged talk of only the most worthwhile of the small comedies and annoyances of everyday life. The Tunisian 'daily', the sister of the negro barman in the hotel whom we had seen on our first evening in the city, spoke only pigeon French and the acquaintances we made in the Café de Paris, who were many and various, rarely spoke English. But that did not matter. I had begun to write *The Unrecorded Life of Oscar Wilde*, a book which I believed of some importance to the history of nineteenth century literature, and this kept me pleasurably busy all day and thanking God for M. Gazère whom I recalled in the first book of this series, and for my own aptitude for languages, which made me happy to talk French at night.

So, as will be guessed by that score or two of readers who unaccountably borrow the books of this series from lending libraries, a routine was soon formed. A set of four back-to-back bookshelves which stretched the width of my too-large room, leaving a sort of gateway between them, divided the dining-sitting room from the study in which I settled down to work, trying to extricate the truth from the countless legends of Wilde, and I would remain at a solid desk for two or three hours. I enjoyed a siesta after lunch as I did for all the years I lived on the Mediterranean and worked again after tea till it was time to bath and change for the evening, not spent in any socially exacting way but at a table in the corner of the Café de Paris, or in the warm weather on the pavement outside it.

The scene at night never ceased to interest me. There never were such people for street eating as the Tunisians. Tunis is a clean city, but before the street sweepers come around in the early hours of the morning it looks as though an army of fruitarian monkeys had passed through. Every few yards there are fruit stalls, which stay open until after midnight, and nut stalls, which offer almonds, peanuts, pistachios, and sunflower seeds. Paper-wrapped sweets are also sold from the pavement, and brightly-lit shops display a wide selection of rich confections—honey cakes, cream cakes, and almond paste. One can buy and eat, messily but contentedly, all kinds of hot vol-au-vents and sausage rolls, for making flaky pastry is a popular art. And it is not only the children who stroll licking ice-cream cones. A fortune would await someone who introduced the toffee apple, familiar in England a few decades ago, or even the fish-and-chip shop. Swordfish steaks wrapped in Arabic newspapers might seem exotic to the Londoner but would, nevertheless, be popular. The Tunisian *boulevardiers* and noctambules were mostly young and they liked talking to foreigners, not only because there was profit to be made from them. They had the blessed gift of unmalicious laughter and delighted in exposing their own absurdities. For instance when a football team had won a match in the afternoon its members and a few hangers-on would roar round the town shouting and singing and generally behaving like rowdies (though not vandals). Those with whom I was sitting would watch me closely to see how this behaviour would strike me, and sometimes ridicule it as infantile, however much they had cheered the team in the afternoon. Likewise when there had been a wedding during the day it was the rather silly custom for the guests and families to pack themselves into motor-cars and drive up and down the avenues continuously pressing their sirens, making an infernal din in streets which were noisy enough already, and a wedding which did not inspire this screeching cavalcade was considered poor. Everyone claimed to disapprove of this, a perverted relic of old Mohammedan customs, though doubtless each forgot this disapproval when he came to his own wedding-day.

There was, too, more drunkenness in Tunis than in most Muslim cities, particularly (as in England) at the week-end. Police were thick on the ground (though the plain-clothes variety were less intrusive than in Tangier) and occasional violence and arrests added to the vital and dramatic night-scene.

I did not spend every evening at the Café de Paris, though I could have done so without much sacrifice, for occasionally I would gather a number of casually chosen friends in the long room of my flat. Once a British ship HMS *Rothesay* came in to the port and a dozen ratings came to drink beer with us. No longer the underpaid and needy matelots I had known for most of my life, they had changed little with prosperity, though they chose Beethoven's Fifth Symphony for the record-player. I still have a cast-iron crest appropriated and painted by one of them and brought ashore in gratitude for the quiet evening in easy chairs which matelots in foreign ports appreciate.

Occasionally visitors from England turned up, usually unexpectedly. Ian Fleming's widow and son came with an artist, and a theatrical producer, Robert Selbie, hired a car with which he took us to see more of Tunisia than we had hitherto had the chance of exploring, including the amphitheatre at El Djer. There was also a young Englishman named Tim Belton who had a yacht with which he sailed about the Mediterranean picking up wealthy passengers, an amusing and profitable way of passing time.

Most pleasant of all perhaps was the visit of Darrell Bates's younger son Nicky who was taking a summer vacational course in Tunis with a number of other undergraduates from English universities. It was twenty years since I had met young men of this type, and more since the days when my brother was at St John's College Oxford, when I shared with him and entered into his enthusiasms and interests. From all accounts, from the fatuous exaggerations of the British media, I would have supposed that the undergraduates of today would have no enthusiasms and very few interests beyond passing necessary examinations, obtaining public gratuities for their support, living with female students or becoming victims of the more dangerous drugs—a picture of monstrous disproportions. Nicky himself and his friends who came not only from the more famous (and once aristocratic) colleges of Oxford and Cambridge, but from redbrick universities and polytechnics, were very much alive and interested in the world about them and if—from the passing of classical education—they had less culture and seemed to emphasize provincial dialect, their knowledge of literature, even of the English literature which preceded the present slump, was heart-warming. Several of them, including Nicky Bates, were engaged to be married or living with a girl, some of them practised one sport or another but most agreed to leave the old kind of fanatical athleticism and rivalry to professionals who intended to dedicate their lives to these. None of them, except Nicky, had read any book of mine but they questioned me closely about the profession of letters. They had charm and good manners and they left me as young men of a very different kind had left me in Las Palmas, re-assured and confident that I had not dropped out of a place in the younger world, as (now in my sixties) I might have expected to do so.

I never, I hope, practised the manners and mannerisms of the *faux jeune*, never tried to use with an air of knowingness their slang and although I looked 'young for my age' never flaunted that painful youthfulness which some ageing men try to cultivate. As in the army when I was among younger and less educated men I remained myself, without talking down or being unnaturally matey, and as in the army this policy of naturalness paid off. I was happy among them and they were completely at ease.

Yet in spite of those meetings with my compatriots it was with Tunisians that I liked to associate and the life of this Tunisian city that I understood. There were few reminders in it of its history before the Arab conquests and only the *medina* with its narrow cobbled streets and a few mosques and gateways which pre-dated the French and Italian occupations of the last hundred years. But Habib Bourguiba, who though a sick man was still revered as the creator of the modern state, had introduced a new liberalism and a freedom for the individual far more easy-going than in other Muslim countries. Only the old and bigoted observed Ramadan and other usages at all strictly, and young Tunisians who had worked in Europe had brought back modes of dress, music, dancing and sport which abandoned the ways of their fathers. There were two daily newspapers in Tunis, one of which had given me, rather to my embarrassment, a headlined welcome when I arrived, and the discothèques were as noisy and the boutiques as way-out as any elsewhere. Even the *hammams*, once the places of religious ablutions, were loud and sociable. It was a city of distinct character, scorned by package tourists but delightful to me and Joseph.

When at last I was installed in my flat, I soon learned enough about Tunisian food to make up for the lack of many things I had enjoyed elsewhere. In Carthage, the second city of the ancient world, the inhabitants of the bright new villas that now occupy the area turn up Roman coins and pieces of pottery from before the time of Christ. So a few miles away in Tunis despite the modernization—towering apartment blocks, continuous traffic, and the Hilton hotel—surely something must remain of the gastronomic traditions of the classical world?

There are. Olives, which were once exported to Rome in the form of oil for cooking and lighting, and figs which Cato gave the Roman senators to arouse their greed, are sold and eaten in the streets of Tunis today, and a recipe devised by the Latin epicure Apicius for cooking sea bream is still used by Tunisian cooks.

But Tunisian cuisine has been enriched over the centuries by the influence of the conquering Arabs. Today *kebabs* are one of its staples, and *cous-cous* is on the menu of every restaurant. Finally and most fortunately, the last century Tunisian cooks have learned finesse from the French colonizers. Thus, in this comparatively small North African country is found one of the happiest combinations of materials (particularly fish and fruit), skilled cooking, and lively appreciation of native dishes.

This culinary richness may not be apparent to the casual visitor or tourist if he is content with the pretentious catering in his newly built luxury hotel. He will be given the largest and most succulent *scampi* to be found anywhere in the Mediterranean, with a very fair mayonnaise. He will perhaps try *cous-cous* made from manufactured semolina and boiled mutton served in a special dish with a plaited cover over it to conserve the full aroma. Or he may be regaled with strawberries Chantilly, for strawberries are plentiful. He may experiment further with such typically Tunisian

specialities as *brik a l'oeuf* and *tajin*. But unless he is entertained in a Tunisian home where there is a cook skilled in
the traditional cuisine of his people, he will not know the
hundred or so spices in the local repertoire, the many
herbs—both dried and fresh, and some of them wild—or
the distillations from flowers: geraniums, orange flowers,
roses, and jasmine, which enliven the delicious sweet
dishes sold by confectioners or made at home.

Nor will the visitors be familiar with the beautiful fish
that are caught off the Tunisian coasts, since many of them
are rarely found elsewhere. The groupers, for instance, that
noble family of spotted creatures with firm, delicately
flavoured flesh, grow to about four feet in length. Or the
eccentric *ange de mer*, also called the angel shark or monkfish,
which is cooked with green peppers. Then there is the
saint-pierre, which we call John Dory; the red and grey
mullets; the *loup de mer* or sea bass; the picturesque *saupe*
with its golden-yellow stripes, the colourful mackerel, and
the snub-nosed *brème de mer* (sea bream or pomfret). *Daurade*,
the gilt-headed bream, which has a golden spot on each
cheek and a crescent-shaped one on its brow, is a prized
fish found only commonly in Tunisian waters. In Tunis it is
usually poached and served with a pale rose-coloured
bechamel, made with the coral of *oursins*, or sea urchins.
(This preparation obviously was introduced by the French,
who are the only people to fully appreciate the spiny little
creatures. In Paris when oysters are out of season *oursins*
take their place on hors d'oeuvre trays.)

So plentiful and so varied is the fish of Tunisia that it is
possible there to make what is often attempted unsuccess-
fully in other places outside the southern coast of France—a
local *bouillabaisse*.

The first truly Tunisian dish I learned to produce was the

celebrated *brik*. This is not at all what it may sound like; it is a paper-thin pastry folded around some morsel, most often an egg sprinkled with herbs, and fried for a moment or two in deep oil. The wafer covers an area the size of a large plate and the egg, or piece of shellfish, or meat, or vegetable, swells it only in the middle. To handle it correctly you must pick it up with the fingers of both hands and nibble your way through the pastry to the prize, an operation that may leave your fingers oily. The process is even more difficult if the egg filling has only been cooked lightly. Then there is *tajin*, which, unlike *tajin* in other North African countries, is a kind of loaf made by pressing together pieces of meat or poultry, eggs, bread crumbs, grated cheese, herbs, and spices. The loaf is later sliced and served hot. *Tajin* is an economical dish, for fine bread crumbs account for part of its volume. But like the bread crumbs in sausages, they are not, or should not be, perceptible. A Tunisian cookery book, a rather magnificent production presented to me by the Minister for Tourism, gave no fewer than a dozen recipes for *tajin*, all of which have diced meat, eggs, and grated cheese but very little else in common, for the housewife makes the mixture according to taste and what she has in her larder. Peas, green or dried beans, tomato puree, mint, artichoke hearts, eggplant, potatoes, and capers can all go into a *tajin*. But whatever the ingredients, there should be a sliceable, well flavoured mass on the outside and served with a piquant sauce.

Where *cous-cous* is concerned, I found that restaurants in Tunisia made little pretence of cooking it with anything but manufactured semolina. The dish may be little the worse for its use of the manufactured product, but *cous-cous*-specialists can appreciate home-made semolina, just as Italian pasta-eaters recognize at once the difference between mass-manufactured spaghetti and the freshly made variety. The Tunisians do not add raisins to the meat, as the Moroccans do, but they serve a peppery sauce called *harissa*, made with dried red peppers.

All forms of kebab (a general term used for anything cooked on skewers over charcoal) are as popular today as they were when the Arabs first introduced them a thousand years ago. Called *brochettes* by the French and *pinchitos* by the Spaniards, the skewered meat that nomadic peoples learned to make palatable by roasting over their campfires has come to be recognized as one of the greatest achievements of world cookery. There is nothing quite like kebabs, not even the roast beef of old England, the glorious grilled steak, or the tender *gigot*. The cubes gain something not only from the spices and herbs with which they are impregnated, but also from the aromas that are diffused during the cooking from the rich smoke that rises as the olive oil drips over the burning charcoal. In any Tunisian restaurant, to order kebabs means to watch the meat, poultry, or fish being stripped from the skewers on to your plate, or sometimes on to a pile of rice. Savouring the fragrant morsels is gastronomic bliss. There are other good dishes. *Shermoula*, fish with sweet-and-sour sauce; *Mechouiya*, tomato and pepper salad which recalls the Andalusian *gaspacho*; and *Kousha*, a sea-bass ragout. For Joseph and me, accustomed to Indian food, it was necessary to send an SOS to my friend Myles Eadon asking him to arrange for quantities of spices, peppers and herbs to make curry to be dispatched from London, for although in the Maghreb spices are used plentifully in food it was impossible to find some of those which Joseph considers essential. But between Indian, Tunisian, French and some English food we fared royally.

5

To each man his fads and preferences in the endless
mutations of living and to me there were several advantages
which Tunis had over Tangier. One was the variety of the
flea-markets. There was one of these on the edge of the
medina which consisted of perhaps twenty stalls or small
warehouses selling nineteenth-century French and Italian
furniture and ornaments, chiefly hideous in the style which
was once popular over most of the continent of Europe,
when we were filling our houses with Victoriana, and nowhere more grotesquely ugly than in the houses of colonials
who had brought their household goods from home and
abandoned them here when they left the country. Possibly
victims of that perversion of that nineteenth-century taste
and proportion which has been promoted in recent years
in England might enjoy themselves searching those stalls
and in a horrified way I did so, though I found nothing
to buy.

But three or four miles out of the city was a more genuine
marché aux puces, an area of stalls for dealers in bric-à-brac,
furniture, old clothes and building materials who had been
expelled from the city for sanitary reasons and followed
their trade, visited only by those who meant to buy rather
than by curious tourists who had watched Arthur Negus on
television and expected to find a Rembrandt or articles of
gold or silver at negligible prices. There were stalls exhibit-
ing hundreds, yes hundreds, of those immense wardrobes
once considered essential to middle-class households and
now largely replaced by built-in cupboards. One of these
had its use in my flat and although the chairs and tables I
found were articles of utility rather than of the least beauty
they were inexpensive. The European pottery, early English

watercolours and silver which had been the collections of my life-time, would make that huge light room in my flat tolerable, however uninteresting was the furniture.

The carpets and rugs I saw were chiefly machine-made and conventional, but one day just as I was leaving the market, I was offered a carpet of an origin I did not immediately recognize. It was handmade of a regular geometrical design of a soft red and black, diced with white, a thing of beauty not least because of its size. As a rug it would have been less significant, but this plain regular pattern carried to twelve feet by eight was impressive and quite lovely. It was in pristine condition yet because of its soft warm colouring did not look new. I asked the price expecting it because of its size and quality to cost at least two hundred dinars (about £175 at that time).

The Tunisian vendor, a keen-looking middle-aged man, said it was thirty-five dinars and I was about to agree but Joseph who had been trained by the uses of the cloth-sellers of Delhi's Chandni Chowk, was quite unable, even in buying a bargain, to agree to any named price without reducing it. He admitted the false economy of wasting time over this when making unimportant purchases but never allowed me to spend, anywhere or on anything, a sum of real significance to our modest finances without trying his skill. He immediately offered the stall-owner twenty dinars and while I examined the carpet entered on a long good-tempered process of parleying. At last twenty-four dinars, just over twenty pounds, was agreed on and the carpet which has brought real delight to me in many settings is under my feet as I write.

This was the sort of incident which made Tunis a civilized and exciting city to me though all Carthage had become a stony waste covered by an excretion of suburban villas.

6

I felt sufficiently settled in Tunis, sufficiently sure that I had found the home I wanted, to visit London which I had not seen since I left Tangier. That I did not regard it, like most who live round the Mediterranean, as a few hours' journey to be made several times a year, was due to the fact that I 'did not fly', as the phrase goes, and had to find means of sea travel from Tangier or go overland by Spain and France. It occurred to me then that whatever caused this, prejudice or fear, was an absurdity. I had only been once in the air when I was flown in the open cockpit of a World War I plane from Buenos Aires to Montevideo by an ex-Air Force officer who was trying to start a regular service between the two capitals. Almost everyone I knew thought nothing of flying in all directions and under any conditions, as Joseph had flown to and fro from India a number of times.

So I resolved to put a stop to this and booked on the next London flight by a plane in regular service.

It was rather a disappointment to a man who expected startling results from every novel experience. I worked on a *Times* crossword as the plane rose into the air and like A. E. Housman at Bredon I could 'see the coloured counties' below me as we approached Gatwick.

After that flight to London I felt that at any moment I could go home on business or pleasure without delay or difficulty and so felt more comfortable entrenched in Tunis. I began to learn more about the place and its past surroundings from Susan Raven's enchanting book *Rome in Africa* and from other sources. Though I could never be a historian or an archaeologist I knew, in the smug phrase, what I liked, and could be carried away by oddments of information about the Carthaginians, Romans, Arabs and French who had successively occupied the country. I re-read *Salammbô* and determined to go to as many places as possible in Tunisia which had known Roman history, from Tabarka (Thabraca) on the north west coast to El Hamma (Aquae Tacapitanae) in the south.

I did not intend to make a book about these, feeling that Susan Raven had left little to be done, but it was delightful to be doing something at last which I should never have to write about, and to enjoy discovery for my own pleasure and interest, without ties or obligations. My first journey was to Tabarka near the Algerian border to which I went by hired car with Nicky Bates, a lively companion. It was a little seaside town like a North African Hythe, the only tourist centre a palatial affair with its own beach two miles away. We stayed in a little Tunisian hotel where we ate shellfish and hare, a happy combination, and were kept awake most of the night by a dance band playing just under our bedroom. The journey back to Tunis was by an intolerably slow train which stopped at every station, taking on noisy parties of young Tunisians with musical instruments who shouted songs and leapt about disconcertingly, railway travel being regarded as an occasion for festivity and fun in that country.

Then I went with Joseph to Sousse, the Roman port of Hadrumetum, down the Eastern coast of the country. Its *cothon* or inland basin had been built by the Phoenicians five centuries BC but allowed to silt up by the Romans who used fewer harbours for their large ships. Sousse today was a cheerful Tunisian city with good hotels and European houses. We looked at one or two of these and decided that if we got tired of Tunis we would move here.

7

Then occurred something which, if I were writing a subjective autobiography, might be considered dramatic, even critical. I had a heart attack.

It happened just as some Tangerine friends had made the difficult journey through Algeria by car to visit me—Anna McKew and her Moroccan friend Nasser and Hugh and Trish Wilton. This brought back my fourteen years in Tangier since they could tell us all the gossip and the usual obituaries, details of esoteric interest, to enjoy which one needed to have lived in the creepy and eccentric little European community of Tangier. At Guitta's, the Gibraltarian restaurant much patronized by the British, the mother of the family had died and as she was also the cook this caused a gap. A character with a certificate in Midwifery given the title of doctor had taken to breaking into tears in public places and 'Scots Mary' had left the town to return to Glasgow. Barbara Hutton no longer called the Fez decorator with whom she had been friendly a 'Vietnamese Prince' and the young Spaniard whom David Herbert referred to by the romantic name of 'Gypsy' was no longer to be seen driving his car. Anne Harbach was becoming nearly blind and although there were bitchy critics who wished it was her voice rather than her sight which was failing, everyone in fact sympathized. Hector Bolitho's brother had died and George Greaves had grown a white beard and looked like a Major Prophet. And so on. This catalogue of trivialities we exchanged on the first evening of the visit of my friends sitting on the pavement outside the Café de Paris in Tunis, as once we had sat outside the Café de Paris in Tangier.

The next day, a Sunday, we drove beyond Sidi-Bou-Said

to find a restaurant overlooking the sea where we lunched—
a pleasant uneventful day. Anna and Trish left me at my flat
and we arranged to meet later in the café.

When they had gone I complained to Joseph that I did
not feel well. In answer to a question—put with quite
unnecessary anxiety it seemed to me—as to what was wrong,
I could only make those idiotic replies most of us do in such
circumstances—I felt 'funny'. I wanted to lie down.

It was not until I heard Joseph (who has almost super-
naturally acute instincts in relation to illness) making an
urgent call to a Tunisian doctor asking him to come at once
that I knew anything serious was amiss. I lay quietly on the
settee aware of a slight discomfort in the region of my chest,
a kind of restriction which I should have dismissed as
indigestion if I had been alone. When I asked Joseph long
after those events what had warned him of my thrombotic
attack he was quite unable to say. He just thought I
needed a doctor and so quietly saved my life.

Dr Benaissa came, at once gave me an injection and a
prescription for medicine to be obtained immediately. He
ordered me to bed, forbade me to move and promised to
come again with a heart specialist in the morning. He did
so, and I was interested, in fact somewhat amused to know
that the specialist was Bourguiba's cardiographer. I do not
know what he read on his chart but an ambulance was sent
for me and I was soon in a cool and empty room in a
French hospital run by nuns, being given oxygen and some
liquid by drops in the veins of my wrist. I still could not feel
very much concerned and had been impatient when carried
in a chair from the ambulance to the bed. I had never had
any illness more serious than my annual bouts of influenza
and found it hard to believe that I had one now. When
Joseph obtained permission to stay in the hospital all night,

E

I attributed his anxiety to nervous but unnecessary concern for me. I was touched but not in the least alarmed. Fat men who depend on their brains and feelings in this agitated and neurotic age seldom get through their lives without cardiac trouble of some kind, frequently something which the layman calls a 'coronary' or a 'heart attack' but which often he does not live to call anything at all. It would perhaps be interesting to the reader then, if I could analyse and describe precisely what I felt and the treatment that was given to me. Unfortunately I can do nothing of the sort. I dislike attempts by those outside the medical profession to use its terminology, believing that doctors must be left with their share of mystique in order to convince the patient. So though I remember what were the effects of this illness, the details of Dr Benaissa's treatment or the medicines which were given me in large quantities remain unknown. I can say only that they were remarkably effective. When the breakdown came to me I looked back for possible presages or symptoms and remembered only that I had once suffered from a mild paralysis of the right arm which I took to be a short-lived attack of writer's cramp and resented only because it meant that I could no longer play darts, the only game at which I ever excelled. I remembered periods of acute anxiety, sometimes economical, and crises like that of 1953 recounted in *The Verdict of You All*. But I could think of nothing in my past life, physical or neurotic, which could account for this sudden loss of energy and well-being, this first real illness in my experience and for a long time I refused to believe it was happening to me. I was impatient, as I always am when extrinsic factors intervene (as when I joined the army, went to prison or had to move house), wishing to get on with my work and cursing these tiresome interruptions. But neither then nor at any of these moments of crisis was I guilty of that most detestable of vices—self-pity. I think—a quite unprofessional belief—that my rapid and complete recovery was in large part due to this. If I had begun to regret that I had not a loving family round me, that I might die a long way from home with my life's work (such as it was) unfinished; if I had lost sleep over the danger of not waking or of being left physically or mentally maimed, I should not have been returning to my own flat in three weeks, or perhaps ever again.

Since I have allowed myself this measure of introspection I may add that the sexual appetite and performance (which had for so long been a major part of my life) were in no way impaired but rather widened in scope so that when I had physically quite recovered I developed some interesting new erotic fantasies which I at once put into practice and have retained these developments ever since in no way restricted, since gerontophilia is a common and eager phenomenon in our time and in any country.

To return to my hospital bed, Dr Benaissa apparently saw the danger of my over-confidence and explained the nature of an infarction and convinced me that I had been seriously if not dangerously ill. When he refused to be optimistic about the complete recovery of which my sanguine nature assured me, I began to feel somewhat anxious, but within ten days I insisted on sitting up and playing Scrabble with Anna McKew and suggesting that she and the Wiltons should not delay departure for Tangier which they had planned days before.

I was given all the compensations and concern which people stricken with sudden illness receive and I felt I obtained them by false pretences. Joseph came every day to the hospital making the long and difficult journey by bus to and fro morning and evening. Tom Morray arranged with the British Library to keep up a perpetual supply of books and all my young Tunisian friends came and sent flowers. All these were new and gratifying experiences for me as were telegrams from my only remaining brother and John Hitchcock and other friends who all offered to fly out if Joseph thought it advisable.

Fortunately he was at last convinced that it was not. The most intelligent and comforting letter came from my friend Patrick Kinross who said in effect that a heart attack of this kind which would slow me down somewhat but lead to a quieter, more settled but no less mentally active life was not at all a bad thing, as several of his friends had found. This was exactly as it turned out. I ceased to smoke in hospital and from an average of ten cheroots and sixty cigarettes a day dropped instantly to nil, and have never smoked again. This was a difficult sacrifice to make, or rather to maintain through the four years that have followed, but not an impossible one, particularly as neither Benaissa nor any subsequently consulted doctor has attempted to deprive me of Scotch whisky which they maintain is a good thing, the very water of life which its Gaelic name implies.

8

Soon after I had returned to the flat in Ibn Khaldoun there was an earthquake. It was not an earth-shattering one which left the city in ruins but in my weakened state after being in hospital it was quite severe enough. Although I gathered afterwards that the tremors had lasted less than thirty seconds it seemed interminable at the time as I watched the light suspended from the ceiling swaying to and fro and felt the whole world shaking. Joseph was with me before it ceased and wanted me to go out in the street but

I felt that if the building was to crash down it would do so on us, whether indoors or out, and stayed in my bed.

It was not surprising to find that events of that night, which happened in the midnight hours, were reported almost casually in the Tunisian daily papers. These were Government controlled and clearly had to play down anything that might deter tourists from coming to spend their money in the country. But to us that earthquake, however minor as earthquakes go, was a startling and memorable experience. Most of the residents in our block of flats drifted down the staircase rather sheepishly looking for someone with an instinct for leadership and finding him in the small person of Joseph who shepherded them into our large room and gave them drinks or coffee. From my bedroom I could hear their slightly hysterical voices until they dispersed in the small hours. It would all have been more easily forgotten if it had not been that two days later, in broad daylight, it was repeated while nobody could explain what these seismic spasms portended.

It was not the effect of them which made me realize that Joseph was in urgent need of a holiday of the only kind which is of any value to him, a visit to his home and family in India. The strain of seeing me through that illness—to him at least nearly fatal—coping not only with me but with all my professional and business affairs, with no-one capable of helping him in these highly personal efforts, had left him nervous and exhausted. This in train set off the reasoning— or was it no more than instinct?—which told me that it was time to leave Tunis since I felt unable just then to face the thought of living alone while not fully recovered during the months that he would be absent.

Once the notion of leaving Tunis entered my mind it grew with speed and with increasing conviction. Two months ago

I had hoped to remain here for life—now I was determined to leave at the end of the quarter. All the disadvantages of the place which had been smothered by my innate optimism and desire for a home rose now to support my intention to leave.

I realized, for instance, that the climate (not of Tunisia but of this marsh-bound city) was anything but temperate and knew that if I was to stay here for another stiflingly hot summer it would be necessary to instal vastly expensive air-conditioning such as I had found in flats in Bombay, while in the winter the streets were swept by chilly winds and rain. Then the expense of living here seemed almost intolerable to me—modest though it would be compared with prices everywhere today—and the perpetual shortages of even the most necessary imports made daily marketing a sort of safari in search of rare articles of food and household usages. (This is a factor which the tourist, who is catered for by hotels with special buying facilities, does not realize.)

There were more personal reasons for wanting to leave, chiefly connected with the flat I rented. The Italian woman who signed the lease was *not*, she explained, the owner but his wife, the owner having left to return to Italy some years ago. This meant that there was no one responsible to whom we could turn to complain of the eight children of a female called a caretaker who had been installed by the owner's brother-in-law when he had occupied my flat. This woman combined fostering and motherhood with apparently full-time prostitution. Under us shop premises had been let to a wireless and gramophone repair shop which meant that the noise and chaos about us were unceasing. As I was engaged on the most taxing portion of my book on Wilde I found the disturbances unbearable.

But even these might have been at least temporarily

endured if it had not been for another threat to our continued existence in the country. Both I and Joseph had received the normal visitor's permits for a stay of three months—the most thought necessary for holiday-makers. When they had expired we had begun a search for more durable documents which, the police informed us, had to be issued by one of the Ministries. Which? we asked. The police made several suggestions but as they had never before been faced with an Englishman, still less an Englishman with an Indian secretary, who demanded merely to reside here and was not employed by a bank or educational authorities, they simply did not know and made many and various suggestions. The Ministry of Education? Of Tourism? Of Foreign Affairs? No Ministry except those in charge of Mining and Agriculture was excluded. We had spent nine hectic days trying at office after office, recommended from one large Government building to another, received with invariable courtesy and chatty talk and many promises but we got absolutely nowhere. It had been a fearsome experience of Tunisian unwillingness or inability to decide or take responsibility and we might have continued for another month if a splendid woman in one of the ministries had not been piqued by competition with male incompetence into suddenly cutting through the formalities and persuading some higher official to take the enormous risk of actually signing papers to give us the right of residence for six months.

This time had now elapsed and when Joseph went to the police for automatic renewal of our permits they told him, with the greatest good humour and politeness, that we should have to go through the whole thing again, this time obtaining a permit from the Minister of Culture, one of the few officials we had not approached before.

This was the last straw. I simply had not the strength or determination necessary for a new pursuit through government offices with more indecisive advice at every turn. I gave up, and booking an air passage to Bombay for Joseph I decided to return to London.

It was with true regret that I left Tunis which had so nearly become a permanent home for me. It was also at considerable expense since all my household goods, furniture, books, early English watercolours and the rest had been settled in the flat after their journey from Tangier. But once decided I did not relent sufficiently to change my plans. I made my third flight and arrived one April evening at the house in 'Little Venice' in which I was to stay till life became calm again. The year was 1971.

Six

Dublin

I remained in London only long enough to see my publishers and agents and to verify in the library of the British Museum some references in my book on Oscar Wilde which was nearing completion. Then I went down to that part of Kent in which I had been born and brought up, to consider the future. I did not yet feel that the possibilities were exhausted of a cheap life in the sun but I could not think where they lay. I considered seriously the idea of Argentina which had been the home of my adolescence, but now seemed too far away, or India of which I had seen enough eight years before to know that for me now life on the plains was too hot and life in hill-stations too expensive. Mexico was a possibility, so was Japan for which I had always hankered, but I suppose I lacked the courage to launch myself into such new and remote surroundings.

So I settled down in the little Gate Hotel in Hildenborough to regain some of my lost physical energy by daily walks to the village and through the fields, to work a little in my bedroom under the eaves of which two pairs of house-martins were building, and tried to make plans.

Meanwhile an assistant master at Tonbridge, my old school, which was only three miles away invited me to come round the buildings whose interiors I had not entered for more than fifty years. So I did that thing which men of all ages do with more or less sentiment and pleasure, went back to the scenes of boyhood. It was not a rueful or even highly emotional experience. This freakishly vivid memory of mine made it almost commonplace, for I entered the small room where H. O. Whitby had presided and saw R. L. Aston's fearful classroom in the tower, and Jerry Smart's torture chamber and the scenes of H. R. Stokoe's soporific teaching, and looked over the notice-board, all as if I should be attending school as usual tomorrow. There were a few changes—the Big School as the central hall had been called, was now aggrandized by public subscription, the library moved and enlarged and the boys less 'Tonbridgian' in type. But I felt completely at home in these surroundings—not in the least a tearful old man remembering 'the boys that were boys when I was a boy'. I recognized the particular smells of each group of classrooms—that of the library had moved with it—and met a number of present-day boys and masters. But there were no surprises. I suppose that a part of me had never outgrown my schoolboy self. The chapel, which I had seen in recent years, still awaited the two spires which would complete its planned resemblance to the chapel of King's College Cambridge, and I did not see where, if anywhere, was the Grubber.

More nostalgic was another visit arranged for me—to my boyhood's home, Cage House, at which I had gazed resentfully from outside on a number of occasions over the years. It had been split into two separate dwellings, the back portion belonging now to a master at the Big School, as Tonbridge has always been called in the town, and the front part now inhabited by a retired master of the same.

I was already aware that the farm which had surrounded the house and which I could endlessly explore as a boy had been erased, every grand old barn of it, and replaced by roads of small houses which stretched amid a forest of television aerials from Dernier Road—which had been the last of Tonbridge—to the top of Shipbourne hill, with their tidy little garages and front gardens. This of course was called a 'good thing' by the people who inhabited them and by those concerned with 'the housing problem' generally, and I suppose I must, though resentfully, agree. I knew that the Big Meadow, thirty acres in size, had provided space for over a hundred dwellings, and that in the nearby wood the pine trees which I had climbed to look for wood-pigeons' eggs (though they had always created a problem for us who observed the rule not to take more than one egg out of three in any nest because pigeons laid only two) had all been cleared to give space for the standardized habitations of humans who bred with less restriction than the pigeons did. I knew that the stream which ran below the hop-gardens, over whose water I had seen a kingfisher skim by in all its gleaming beauty, had been dried up or deflected long since and that the barns in which I had hidden to make love concealed on stacks of straw were no more.

But I had not realized the hideous desecration of my home itself. Cage House, a Queen Anne farm-house which should have qualified for preservation as a superb period piece, had stood in two acres of garden which had been cultivated for centuries and had magnificent trees in it, an immense Cedar of Lebanon with bark so soft that pieces of it could be shaped with a pen-knife, a Monkey Puzzle tree

(*Araucaria araucana*) taller than the house, a Whiteheart cherry tree in which I could climb and be reproved by my father, not for eating cherries of which there were too many, but for spitting the stones on the lawn to damage the mower. There was also a walnut tree which bore a hundredweight of nuts most years and peach trees growing on the tall south wall dividing the garden from the farmyard. All this had gone, together with the greenhouse in which a vine grew from which hung ponderous clusters of sweet white grapes and the shrubbery on the kitchen side of the house. Barely a quarter-acre of ground was left around the house and the little gardens of houses jostled the bare lawns on which our mighty trees had stood. Whereas we had been able to look from our upstairs windows to see the Medway two miles away, the windows of the building estate came up to stare back at Cage House which was now anomalous, anachronistic and naked where it stood unwalled and resented by its flashy little neighbours.

By the kindness of the present owners of the 'back half' of the house I saw the room which had been made of our brick-floored kitchen and the brick oven in which we had baked ambrosial bread. I went up to the smart comfortable bedrooms on the second floor which had been attics occupied by Doris, our cook (whom I had made love to in the woods when I was twelve years old), and by servants immemorially when this was a busy farm house. In the 'front half' I sat in the room where we had played bagatelle and climbed incredulously to the top floor on which Richard Blake Brown and I had made an 'oratory' as recounted in *The Altar in the Loft*. But enough of these reminiscences. Poor Richard whose untiring gaiety and kindliness had been overcome in his last years by alcoholism, had died through an accident caused by too much drink two years earlier and

our 'oratory' had become a well-appointed bedroom which
looked out on more rows of identical houses. The present
owners of 'the front part' of Cage House, who knew my
book about it, had found under the floor-boards a highly-
coloured Italian printed portrait of an obscure Saint, his
halo heavily gilt and his cope of purple, which would in
those days have been recognized by me as one of the
liturgical colours. They were kind enough to give me this as
they poured out for me a generous whisky at the end of my
tour of recollection. I was not saddened by this but I
recognized at last that the house which had been the most
beloved home of my boyhood had been restored beyond
hope and I must be satisfied with having memorialized it in
writing, knowing that in all but the rattling skeletons of
mere fact it no longer existed.

2

I had only three months in which I could stay in England
and I had to make up my mind about the future. It came to
me, as the cliché expressively has it, in a flash. I would go to
Ireland. By an intelligent and beneficent piece of legislation
far beyond the foresight or imagination of any British
Government, there was no income tax there to be paid by
professional writers or artists, and the climate, I argued,
could not be worse than that of England. The countryside
was beautiful and during the only visit I had made to
Ireland (to Kilkenny in 1938) the people had seemed
amiable and humorous, not the musical-hall comic lispers in
whom the English still believed, but friendly and easily
pleased. Dublin, I thought was an almost entirely Georgian
city and literature throve there. Besides, there was still time
to make additions or revisions to my book on Wilde and I

wanted to see his country homes in the West. I fondly believed that life cost less there than in England and that small homes were easily found. It was a Catholic country in which, I argued, both I and Joseph would be at home and 'the troubles', if any (it was August 1971), would be confined to the North.

So without much fuss and with no attention at all to warnings, I decided at least to make an exploratory journey, without even at this late juncture in my life recognizing that such is my gift of self-persuasion and belief that my choice is right, that I should not return. So I went into a travel agent's in Tonbridge to arrange the journey.

I decided to go via Liverpool and stay the night in the Adelphi Hotel, an unnecessary expense but one which would satisfy certain other sentimental curiosities of mine. In a chapter called *The Folk that Live in Liverpool* in the third book in this sequence, *The Drums of Morning*, I told how as a seventeen-year-old employed as an assistant master in a preparatory school in the Wirral Peninsula I had come across on the ferry to Liverpool and how that city had been a Great Metropolis to me then, and how I had fed my own longing for sophistication and self-assurance by going into the Adelphi Hotel. So now I asked myself whether a young man of today could possibly give himself high-flooding pleasure by walking into a large hotel like the Adelphi, sitting alone at a table in a grandiose gallery and after checking that his money was sufficient for any eventuality *ordering tea*? The slabs of marble and gilded cornerpiece, the thick carpets and the faultless linen of the well-trained waiters, the silvery tray and teapot and milk jug, the toast, the little sandwiches and cakes would surely seem to him so much waste of time and he would ask why he was wearing this ridiculous suit and tie and collar when he might be in

jeans on his scooter with a girl behind him and a couple
of benzedrine tablets in his pocket.

I went on to admit that to me Sunday afternoon in the
great reception rooms of that outsize hotel, with enough
money to tip the cloakroom man to keep my shabby blue
mackintosh and felt hat, meant a world of luxury such as I
had known only in the novels of William le Quex, in which
millionaires crossed the Atlantic in luxury liners and ran
nonchalantly from Monte Carlo to Cairo in yachts, while
creamy-skinned women wore the diamonds they bought
with such prodigality. At least, that is as I see myself, alone,
shabby and determined, marching up to the entry and finding my way at last to a table in a large gallery reserved for
tea, with an orchestra playing discreet violin music from a
palm court somewhere below. The moment at which, tea
finished, I lit my Turkish cigarette and gave myself to
dreams of luxuries to come, was a moment of great bliss.

I wanted in this Spring of 1971 to see again what had
given me those tremors of lonely excitement half a century
ago, daring to visit my own past as I had done in Cage
House. So I travelled by train from London to Liverpool.

Will I be believed if I borrow a word from television
commercials and say this was a 'special' visit? I had been
through Liverpool a number of times since then—particularly during the war when I was sent there on a motor-cycle
as a newly created sergeant in Field Security and had been
robbed of my pocket-case while sleeping in the YMCA
there and seen the city recently bomb-scarred and dreary.
But those wartime visits did not interrupt my view straight
back to the Sunday afternoons of 1921. It was for those that
I travelled to Liverpool and came to the Adelphi Hotel.

It was incredibly, almost uncannily the same. Tea was
served in the immense lounge on the ground floor instead

of in the gallery round it, but the tea with toast and jam (at this time alas, uneaten by me) was served by an immaculate waiter, inheritor of those who had brought their trays to me.

Not that I imagined myself, or wished to do so, to have achieved the kind of success that the patrons of that hotel seemed to me to be enjoying long ago. Then it was the goal of all my efforts to be rich and famous, to possess my share of the places in the world reserved for the wealthy and eminent. I had not lost ambition, only changed its direction. I had recognized that I should never be a financially successful writer, should never write a best-seller or win a literary prize, should in fact count myself lucky if I could continue to keep alive to the end by writing, as I had managed to do, sometimes with difficulty, since my first poems were published. But I wanted, passionately, to finish this sequence of books and see it published as a whole under the title which I had learned from the words in dull gold letters on my first Tonbridgian schoolbook *Lyra Heroica*, A book of Verse for Boys, Selected and Arranged by W. E. Henley. A battered copy of this inscribed 'R. C. Cooke, Bought at Pound, Lent Term 1915' is beside me today as it has remained for close on sixty years. On its front cover are just discernible the words from Sir Walter Scott

Sound, sound the Clarion, fill the fife!
To all the sensual world proclaim,
One crowded hour of glorious life
Is worth an age without a name.

The Sensual World gave me a title for the series, in spite of the fact that the *Oxford Dictionary of Quotations* attributes the four lines not to Sir Walter Scott, as printed after the words on *Lyra Heroica*, but (with a slight variation) to Thomas Osbert Mordaunt (1730-1809).

But to return to the ambition I recognized on my way to Ireland in 1971, it had lost most of its materialism and centred itself on finishing *The Sensual World* series, on *The Unrecorded Life of Oscar Wilde* which I believed was the first objective view of the subject, and on making enough money to keep myself without acute want and leave to Joseph as much as I could towards repaying him for thirty years of his life given to me and my work. If that is vaulting ambition I was guilty of it but it seemed moderate enough to me. As for fame, publicity, recognition and the like I was—and I sincerely thank God for it—no longer interested in them, except solely and strictly as a means to the second of these two aims.

3

I knew almost nothing about the city of Dublin except stories told me by Sean O'Casey, chiefly of the Easter Rebellion and his part in the Irish Republican Army of that time. So I put up at a pub on Eden Quay named with ridiculous trans-atlantic pretentiousness the Waldorf Astoria. It overlooked the River Liffey, turbid and reeking at that point, in a region of slummy streets and warehouses which, as I soon learned, alternated in Dublin with superb Georgian architecture.

'I began to 'get the tone' of the place. I had been given letters of introduction by Harford Montgomery Hyde addressed to various important citizens, the lawyer son of Oliver St John Gogarty, Desmond Guinness who fought for the preservation of Georgian architecture, a writer named Ulick O'Connor and several others but I made no use of these then or thereafter (except in the case of Ulick O'Connor) being determined to explore and come to know something of Dublin for myself. It seemed to me a grave and unaccountable deficiency in my life that I had reached my sixties without becoming acquainted with this city, perhaps the most characterful of all those I had seen. I did not want to compare it with London, Buenos Aires or Bombay, or any place in my own country or abroad that I knew, for I recognized that comparisons in this case were useless. I wanted to collect innumerable small impressions, vistas perhaps unattractive to its own people or its visitors, but which in my own experience would make a whole.

It was first of all a city of contrasts, hideous squalor and graceful architecture, brilliant conversation and drunken stupidity, beauty in face and figure and unkempt ugliness which made one turn away. It was an amorous city—men and women, boys and girls linked in its streets wherever one looked, a noisy argumentative alcoholic city, every bar filled from early morning till late at night with unceasingly disputative males pausing only in their contentions to swallow their pints. It was a grim and forbidding city when its eternal sunlessness enveloped it, yet it could break into light and laughter in unexpected flashes.

Architecturally its beauty lies not so much in its particular buildings but in its long superb streets planned and built in the eighteenth century, crowded in though they are with clumsy Victoriana. O'Connell Street itself, reputed to be the widest city street in Europe, was impressive to me for I love such great city streets everywhere, the Champs Elysées, Kingsway, and the huge thoroughfares between buildings in the cities of South America and South Africa—a vulgar taste I am told and one which owes its origin perhaps to my own upbringing during which I never saw a wide street till I went to Paris at eighteen.

But I love, too, open spaces in the hearts of cities, great

plazas and parks, the Connaught Circle in Delhi, the Grand Place in Brussels, the Piazza San Pietro in Rome and the rest, and the most affectionately remembered if not the most beautiful of all, St Stephen's Green in Dublin, where on rare days of summer sunlight a band plays and young people escaping from the offices and shops stroll happily, while round the Green there are still shops selling articles of quality such as one must search for arduously in London.

It is a prosperous city now but full of reminders of what cataclysmic differences between the rich and poor there had been under British rule in past centuries. I believe accounts of the ferocious poverty, lust and crime of the old East End of London, for these are recorded, but in Dublin I could actually see evidence of what had been as lately as Sean O'Casey's day, and in some respects persisted even now.

Above all it was for me, however interesting and friendly, a grey city, a city almost without colour except in shop windows and on the posters of cinemas. The river and canals seemed to have thick brown water, the sky seemed eternally clouded, even the sea as one saw it on the way to suburbs was lustreless and dingy. All that one saw in Dublin, every glimpse of beauty and delight, lacked luminosity and variegation and one was forced to feel every day how attractive this place could be *if only* it was in the sun.

Even the bright faces and laughter of young people, so liberally displayed in Dublin, were no compensation for this.

4

However I had not come to Dublin for the sake of the climate but, among other things, to fill a disgraceful gap in my knowledge of European countries. So I wandered about contentedly for several weeks until I felt I should look for a home. The only part of Dublin in which I wanted to live, the streets overlooking or around St Stephen's Green, was out of the question because of the near-impossibility and expense of finding any kind of accommodation there. An estate agent sent me to see a furnished flat to let in Dun Laoghaire, the former port of Kingstown, seven or eight miles South. I went by train not knowing that frequent buses ran out to the town and looked over the premises described as a 'garden flat', which means in that country of euphemism a basement with or without steps leading up to a back or front yard. Or more frequently, a room or two undivided from the rest of the house with 'access to' kitchen and bathroom. The place I saw was ill-furnished and chilly and had a subterranean smell of dampness which drove me out at once.

However, at the railway station I found that I had to wait forty minutes for a train and went across to the nearest bar, that of the Elphin Hotel, for a drink. This turned out to be one of those fateful chances which changed at least one year and in some senses very much more of my life, for there I found a large room miscalled a lounge bar—fake-antique and funny though it might be considered, but welcoming to me with its immense log fire and that peculiar atmosphere, known to each of us aware of such nebulous things, as that of a good pub. I found, moreover, that the hotel was, in an unpretentious way, residential, saw a clean light dining-room, and booked a room for the following Monday. I remained there for three months and from that pub found a home for the next fifteen months which might have been mine till today.

5

Dun Laoghaire (pronounced Doon Lay-reh) was a busy little seaside town rather like New Brighton on the Mersey estuary, with a windy promenade beside the cold colourless sea and shops like Woolworths and Lipton's in its main street. Its pavements were made almost impassable by perambulators and push-carts propelled by innumerable mothers with more progeny following them, since the population explosion in Ireland continues not in occasional bursts but continuously like machine-gun-fire, and evidence of it makes it difficult to walk the streets till after nightfall. But the town though grey and Victorian is not cheerless. The mailboats come in from Holyhead and bring a cosmopolitan rout who carry their great packs to houses promising bed and breakfast, before they tramp off into the interior. The Martello Tower at Sandycove in which James Joyce stayed for a time and depicted in *Ulysses* still stands, and there are remains of the time when 'Kingstown' was a select home of the English, like the three yacht clubs, one for Protestants, one for Catholics and one for undenominational snobs. These were loud with the accents of West Britons and English-educated Irish.

I settled in and sent a cable to Joseph to tell him that I had found a promising home at last. While I was waiting for him a strange and enchanting thing happened, strange because at my age I did not expect to be treated with confidence and friendship by young men still in their teens or early twenties, who are generally supposed to be intolerant of all mature males. I certainly did not expect to become one of a particular crowd of these adolescents most of whom had known one another since childhood.

One afternoon three youngsters at the bar of the Elphin

were testing one another's eyesight by seeing who could read small type farthest away. I became drawn into this and being peculiarly long-sighted defeated them all. We continued to talk over the pints of Guinness on which they all seemed to sustain themselves and I mentioned that I had to move into the house next door where I had rented a room with a bathroom, and that I intended to put in stocks and utensils that afternoon. At once two of them, Dermot Baker a gay mischievous boy whose father had an immensely prosperous pub, and Owen Burke, a tall young undergraduate studying for the Law, whose nickname for some obscure reason was Squealch, volunteered to help me. They took over the entire proceedings and having filled two trolleys from a supermarket they calmly pushed them out into the street like perambulators and down the road to the Elphin. Such resourcefulness and impudence, and such generosity to me who would have found great difficulty in obtaining the things I needed, won my heart, especially as they afterwards returned the trolleys to the shop. All this was carried out with great good humour and occasional bursts of hilarity, yet with efficiency. That evening several more of their crowd, whose number was strictly limited, joined them in the bar and I shall introduce them here by name, since they meant so much to me and to this book. There was, that night or on some following occasion, Denis Calthorpe who in spite of his English-sounding name was perhaps the most Irish of them all, Rowley Fitzgerald, the son of a famous surgeon, Brian Hamilton a young artist, Padraic Halligan who intended to be an architect and paid his way through the University by doing hard physical labour in England during the summer vacation, Norman Hayden the least businesslike of them who had been conscripted into commerce, Philip Kelly who had

English blood but did not like being reminded of it, Kenneth Maher the only Protestant in the crowd but none the less Irish for that. There was also Ray O'Donnell, known as Billy, who had travelled more adventurously than the rest and bummed his way about the States, and finally Peter Willis who had been at Rossall but had lost none of his Irishness in the process.

These were eleven but they were neither disciples nor a football side. They adopted me, who could have been their grandfather, not as a mentor or sugar daddy to be appealed to for information or a loan, but as one of themselves, sharing their generous code, introduced to their parents and girl-friends. It was more than forty years since I had been accepted by a similar crowd, all natives as they were of a single place, in that case San Isidro, and then I had been of an age with them. This was virtually a new experience and a very exhilarating one.

Not, of course, that it passed without notice in the gossipy little town of Dun Laoghaire. The boys told me with great amusement that some of their parents had shown signs of alarm, which was natural enough remembering that Catholic communities are often more puritanical than the Puritans. There was also a plain-clothes policeman who came frequently to the pub and watched our group suspiciously. I was inclined to be indignant about this for I have never lost my distrust of the fuzz whether called policemen or gardai, but the boys told me with much hilarity that he was a harmless ass who, perhaps because all the boys had long hair, suspected them of taking pot or even the hard stuff, and me of selling it to them. 'Rupert the pusher' was a suggestion which kept them amused for a long time. The boys rather enjoyed all this as they enjoyed flouting the embargo of the proprietor of the Elphin against all who wore their hair long, an embargo which was lifted for them perhaps because they were not rowdies by nature and spent prodigally on pints.

One of their crowd was married, Peter Willis having a splendid little son named Jason, and most of them had girl-friends who were changed around among them so that I never knew when we met in the evening who was 'going with' whom. The girls all had the exquisite complexions and limpid eyes which, as countless visitors have noted, are common to Irish girls; they all drank ale or Guinness from pint glasses and they all kissed me in a generous nepotic way when we parted at night.

The humour of these young people was not my humour—indeed I sometimes think that what makes each race laugh is what most notably divides the Irish from the English, but it was youthful irresponsible humour, free from mockery or self-consciousness. The Mediterraneans are laughter-loving but not very humorous people and I had not enjoyed that curiously elusive inspiration to laugh outright for years. 'The crowd' made me a very happy man.

Then again I had a fall, not metaphorically but a sudden, painful and temporarily crippling tumble. Out of the dining-room of the Elphin hotel three steps descended to an ill-lit passage and they had been covered by a carpet of a continuous pattern on all levels, the result being at that time that they were virtually invisible to one leaving the well-lit dining-room.

Doing so one morning I stepped into space and went full-length to the ground. I was helped to my feet but promptly fainted. I had not done this since once during choir practice at Tonbridge when I had to be picked up and carried away by a school hero named Bill Porter, Captain of Rowing, who afterwards rose to be a Brigadier and CBE. That had been memorable, this was merely painful and rather frightening since I was, as one of the boys ambiguously said, in my *soixant-neuvième* year.

A doctor was summoned and sent me to a local hospital for an X-ray and there, feeling dizzy and weak and unable to protest, I was left waiting on a bench for nearly three hours. Will it seem unfair if I complain that this in my experience seems to be the usual treatment at hospitals, English and Irish, in the case of a casualty not actually in danger of death but urgent enough to be attended to without delay? By the time the proprietor of the Elphin had arrived and persuaded someone to discover whether I was in anything more than acute pain, I was all in. As it turned out no bones were broken and although I was disabled for a time and have walked ever since with a stick, my heart was not affected. I should add in fairness that after long correspondence and delay my solicitors settled with the Insurance company involved for £500 damages. I would very much rather the thing had not happened.

So throughout July and August I spent most of my time sitting in the bar of the Elphin, with my leg up surrounded by my young friends, idle except for conversation which for me can never be a purposeless way of passing time.

6

Then by that almost superstitiously respected good fortune of mine in the matter of house property, I found a home. On the outskirts of Dun Laoghaire was a region of Municipal housing, uniform streets of semi-detached villas, called by the Hibernian regional name of Sallynoggin. Isolated from this by huge trees planted in the eighteenth century was a large grey Regency house, its name in turn derived from the area it had once dominated—Glenageary. Its rooms were fifteen feet high and its hallway alone could have been cut up by modern methods of conversion into four flats but its owners had done little rebuilding inside or out, simply sealing up doorways and putting in bathrooms to make about ten large flats of the huge old mansion, which had once stood in several miles of open country. The many stables and out-houses had also been converted into flats and the great kitchen garden sold to a nurseryman, but the open meadow before the house and the long drive approaching it from the road had been left intact and still had the spacious grace of their period.

In this house, I heard, a flat on the first floor was to let, its occupant having been given living quarters at his place of employment and wishing to break his lease. It was a very odd-shaped part of the building divided haphazardly from the rest but completely self-contained. There were windows thirteen feet high in rooms not ten feet across, there was a passage twenty-five feet long leading from the front door to two rooms beyond the neighbouring flat, but in its strange way it had a period dignity about it and from its windows one looked over its grounds and saw nothing of the modern slums which surrounded it. I went to see it on the day after it was put up to be let, enquired only the rent which was £10 a week and took it at once. My furniture, sent from Tunis to an English warehouse, would arrive before the end of September and Joseph at about the same time.

He in the meantime had suffered a loss which not only distressed but infuriated me. His elder brother Anthony, a married man with seven children who was a teacher in a Catholic orphanage eight miles away from Belgaum where I had first met him and Joseph, was cycling home from work when he was knocked off his bicycle by a car. The motorist drove on and left him lying in the road and was never identified, so that no compensation was paid by the State or anyone else to the widow. I say this infuriated me and it did more than that, reminding me how impotent are the poor in what we smugly call 'underprivileged' parts of the world and how recently and inadequately we have improved on this in Europe. For Joseph it was a shocking loss, for he was summoned by a neighbour who had chanced to hear of the accident. He ran the mile to where it had taken place with two friends, a Hindu and a Christian, and found his brother unconscious still by the roadside from which no one had bothered to remove him. Joseph held up a car and got his brother to hospital but Anthony died without recovering consciousness.

For Joseph this meant, not only grief for a dearly loved brother but the responsibility, which he instantly and willingly assumed, of supporting his brother's widow and younger children, the ties and obligations in an Indian family being of a nature which only Jews in the West can fully understand. Since I can afford to pay him nothing commensurate with the value of his work this meant, and will mean for the foreseeable future, the total abandonment of every minor luxury or entertainment in his life, but did not mean that he failed to return to me.

My furniture and books arrived a few days before he did and I thanked God for the friendship of my young Irish friends. Without request or reward they gave up whole days of their summer holiday to do the very considerable work of carpet-laying, picture-hanging, book-shelving, decorating and settling my things in those tall rooms, arranging for the disposal of the waste packing and cleaning the floors and windows—all those wearisome chores which are particularly difficult to undertake for someone else's benefit. That they would accept no form of recompense was not so much, I like to think, a matter of pride—rather of unconscious principle. Having accepted me as one of themselves they did for me what they would have undertaken for any of their group who needed it and indeed did undertake for Peter Willis when he found a flat for himself and his wife a few months later.

They went further. When Joseph, whom of course they had never seen, was due to arrive at Dublin airport at the end of September they volunteered with the use of Rowley Fitzgerald's car, to take me to meet him. His plane was four hours late through some delay in Rome and eventually arrived in the small hours of the morning. I remember with the kind of gratitude which honest-to-God unselfishness inspires how five of them sat about the airport long after all bars were closed for no other reason than that they had agreed to do a favour and could not be deflected from it, a kind of generosity of purpose which I sometimes think belongs notably if not exclusively to the youth of Ireland.

Thereafter settled into the flat in that strange gothic great building with all my things around me, with a 'daily' to deal with its gaunt rooms and with Joseph to type for me again I could correct the proofs of the Wilde book, write a novel, watch coloured television and fall into a blissfully placid routine. Several times a week one or another and sometimes half a dozen of the boys would come out to the house with or without their girl-friends and sit round the log fire drinking beer—Guinness having to be *draught* Guinness and therefore for bar-drinking only. They might bring records they had just bought or fish-and-chips from a nearby shop, or sometimes Peter's baby, or a new friend curious to meet the Englishman and Indian of whom one or another of them had talked. They had wide, one might almost think universal

connexions and they coerced friends or parents of many
callings into kindness to us whom they regarded as unable
to do things for ourselves, so that one of their fathers who
had to go to London took with him a watercolour of mine
for sale at Christie's and another who worked in the Dublin
branch of Philips carried out a tricky repair to a record-
player which had defeated the Philips branch, the STIET in
Tunis. Only someone as impractical as I who had lately
given up driving a car and who was also alone in a strange
country will understand what this kind of considerateness
meant.

So life would have been both hopeful and pleasant if it
had not been for my growing awareness that never since I
had arrived in Ireland had there been a really warm fine day.
I boasted that I had learned indifference to the climate and
expected the grey skies of Ireland but when in October the
evenings began noticeably to close in and people admitted
that the summer was gone I realized that I had scarcely seen
the sun since I left Tunis. This began to depress me and
Joseph, though neither of us wanted to admit it. What made
it more irritating was that at the palest streak of sunshine
everyone in Ireland shouted 'Lovely morning!' or 'It's a
grand day, isn't it?' and talked of 'all that lovely weather in
July' or something of the sort.

7

The only friends I had in Dublin were well-off Irish people
who had come to Tangier to find the very sunlight I was
missing and one of them who owned a cinema invited me
to come to the Horse Show, that tremendous occasion when
the whole country seems at its most traditional and attrac-

tive. I watched England beaten in the Show Jumping by half a point by the German team and found myself moved by emotions which I had thought long since forgotten. I was glad to have witnessed it that year (1971), the last in which 'the situation' was considered safe enough to allow us to compete, and glad to notch up another of those heavily publicised displays at which I have, through one or another chance of time and place, been privileged to be present in person—the Men's Finals at Wimbledon, Henley before the war, the Oxford and Cambridge Boat Race and the Cup Final at Wembley. It was as exciting and as alien as the passion and exultation of any of these had been to me, who knew so little of them.

At that Horse Show I met a man named Paul Rowan who had inherited a great seedsman's business in Dublin, was something of a poet and as a conversationalist was given to gigantic exaggerations and lively narrative. He invited me to dinner at one of the three yacht clubs of Dun Laoghaire— the most West British of them—and when he heard that I had almost completed a book about Wilde he told me that he had a house on Lough Corrib which adjoined Moytura, the home of Oscar's father. Would I like to come down to it and see whether I could pick up any extant relics or stories of Wilde?

It was not so much for the sake of the book that I gladly went—for I felt I had already discharged my obligations to Oscar by compelling, as a subsequent biographer has said, 'some careful rethinking on the use of familiar sources and the re-telling of familiar anecdotes', in other words wiping the slate clean of much of the silly nonsense which the story of Wilde had accumulated. It was for the visit itself that I went, to the west coast, to the mountains and lakes, to the country of legends, not expecting to learn anything of much use to me as a biographer. I knew where Moytura House stood and I remembered that Oscar had written to his friends from a fishing lodge on Lough Fee which was farther west, but what could be found of interest in them nearly a century after his few visits?

We set out from Dublin on Friday October the first. We drove almost due west and came to an inn on the shores of Galway Bay which was famous in a particular Irish way. It was known to people all over the country who came there to eat oysters which were sold daylong by scores of dozens and were of such supreme excellence that I for one found them—on that day at any rate—superior to the finest Whitstable or Colchester oysters I had eaten. I admit that none of us is guiltless of superlatives derived from the place or occasion; we are all apt to believe and that some little *vin du pays*, drunk on an evening when we happened to be enthralled by the surroundings or events, was better than a great wine drunk in a merely luxurious restaurant. There was nothing 'olde' or even picturesque about the pub and the wind outside was blustery and the sky and water of an uninviting grey. But those oysters, handed across the gloomy bar of an ill-lit pub and swallowed with draught Guinness while unremarkable customers blew pipe-smoke over us, were the most delectable I have ever eaten. I say this in defiance of the opinion or silence on Galway oysters of most text-books—Larousse talks of *Marennes*, those pitiful drops of jellified sea-water, and the *Encyclopaedia Britannica* says of the Galway seashore that early potatoes are raised there in deep sea-sand, but neither of them mentions the divine shellfish. We ate a dozen each and went on to Paul Rowan's home between the grounds of Moytura House and the Lough and found a blaze of scented drift-wood in the open fireplace.

That evening, fortified with Scotch whisky—since the Irish rarely carry their patriotism to the point where they enjoy the local product—I prepared to face my first Galway 'character', believing him to be one of many sought out by tourists, and though Synge wrote in another dialect I expected him to be a sort of *Playboy of the Western World*. He was in fact the son of that employee of the Wildes of whom Oscar wrote to a prospective tenant of his fishing lodge— 'my servant, an excellent fisherman and his wife a good cook, are in charge of it'. But Frank Houlihan, born long after Sir William was dead and Oscar had ceased to visit Ireland, knew nothing of the writer or his family and had only a few dim old memories inherited from his own father. He told some Galway folk tales which might suggest to a literary historian who considered Wilde's early talents were important enough to study, that his fairy tales owed something to this countryside. But nothing more.

I was therefore feeling somewhat disheartened next morning when we set out to find the Wildes' fishing lodge on Lough Fee, motoring by the road on which Oscar must have travelled by pony trap with his friends in 1877, and as I wrote in *The Unrecorded Life of Oscar Wilde*, passed through what Oscar called some of 'the most romantic scenery in Ireland' with the Maamturk mountains and the Twelve Pins ahead of them. Romantic, certainly, but grey, grey—I have to repeat the word—a bleak morning which would have been glorious with sunlight on the hills and lakes.

But Illaunroe itself was no disappointment. A tongue of woodland ran out into the lake on which stood an old neglected house almost overgrown by a forest of *ponticum* rhododendrons. It was unoccupied and silent but for a low splashing where the lake lapped its banks and landing-stage. Anomalously and timorously a lonely black-faced sheep seemed to come out of the undergrowth but would not let us approach her. The whole effect was eerie and wistful.

No student of Wilde's life has ever recorded a visit to Illaunroe and when we found the female caretaker at a cottage two miles away she knew nothing of the old fishing lodge except that it was sometimes let to anglers in the season. But before we left the dripping trees around it by the single track which led to the mainland from the peninsula on which the house stood, Paul Rowan insisted on peeping in the glass-fronted main door and called me to see what he had found.

In front of us there was an arch across the narrow hallway and over it was a mural showing two naked cherubs, each with rod and line, one of them on the left of the arch jubilant with large fish at his feet, the other, on the right side, tearful. Beneath them were the words TIGHT LINES printed in letters of a form I recognized. At once I realized that I was seeing a pale relic of the work of Frank Miles who had stayed here in 1876 and lived with Oscar in London. He had decorated the walls of the church at Bingham when his father was rector there and painted portraits of Society women in just this style when he and Oscar had shared ambitions. The printed words were exactly as he wrote his name on the only existing portrait of himself reproduced in my book (and later in that of Mr Martin Fido).

It was, perhaps, a trivial discovery—but a genuine one. So Frank, who died insane after he and Oscar had parted, had occupied himself with painting these half humorous figures while Oscar was fishing. To his friend 'Kitten' (Reginald Harding) Oscar wrote in August 1876 from Moytura House: 'Frank has never fired off a gun in his life (and says he doesn't want to) but as our proper sporting season here does not begin till September I have not taught

F

him anything. But on Friday we go into Connemara to a
charming little fishing lodge we have in the mountains
where I hope to make him land a salmon and kill a brace of
grouse. I expect to have very good sport indeed this season.
Write to me there if your claws have not been clipped.
Illaunroe Lodge, Leenane, Co. Galway.' To William Ward
(Bouncer) he wrote a few days later from Illaunroe Lodge
itself: 'I have Frank Miles with me. He is delighted with [it]
all.' Of how delighted he was the evidence was looking
down on me in faded colours from the wall, unrecognized
as more than a facetious memento of fishing painted by
some occupant of the old lodge. I was—there is no other
word—thrilled by the discovery and arranged for photographs to be taken of *Tight Lines* and held up the printing
of my book so that they could be included in it. My gratitude
to Paul Rowan was such that I dedicated the book to him
and his wife.

After our return to Dublin he gave me a more substantial
reminder of our visit to the west. He had a shoot near North
Slob in County Wexford to which each year great quantities
of white-fronted Geese (*Anser albifrons*) came from Green-
land. Paul was a sportsman and a good shot and although
free from the sentimentalism of Paul Gallico and his *Snow
Goose*, very strictly limited the number of wild geese he
allowed to be brought down by himself and other members
of the syndicate who rented the shoot. When he sent me one
item from his bag of the previous week I had no conflicting
morals in the matter, though I had long realized that I was
torn in these things, an animal-lover who has gone to bull-
fights since young manhood, a gourmet who eats shot
pheasants and partridges while he is feeding small birds
throughout the winter, and most paradoxical of all (since I
am horrified by the idea of tearing out the gullets of fish)

a devoted consumer of trout and salmon. I will not enter
into polemics on these things but admit that while I myself
have almost the fastidious abhorrence of a Jainite of killing
all living creatures I have no scruples about eating anything,
except animals or birds which have been deprived of sunlight
and movement throughout their lives to tickle the appetite
of mankind, battery-fed chickens or anaemic calves.

To return to that wild goose, it was the first time in my
life as an admitted—even a professional—gourmet that I
had ever cooked and eaten this bird and sublimely satisfying
I found it. With none of the fishiness of wild duck or the
lardaceous fatness of the domestic goose it was rich and
gamy, tender and succulent, with a memorable flavour
cooked *à la bourguinonne*. It was the only remarkable food I
had in Ireland which I had imagined to be a land overflowing with milk and honey, or at least creamy butter and
heavenly home-made bread. There were a few faked *haute
cuisine* places in Dublin in which to eat at outrageous prices
but in bourgeois restaurants and homes the food, heated-up
products of the supermarket, was no better than in England.
Smoked salmon cured in the country, oysters in Galway and
this wonderful wild goose were the only foods of distinction
I found.

8

It may seem strange that I record no reactions, either of
myself or others, to the troubles of Ulster, or about 'the
Irish Rebellion in the North' as my young friends preferred
to call it. The truth is that I tried to shy away from that
complex and unhappy situation. When I cannot be a partisan
in any warfare, as I could be in the anti-Nazi struggle, I am
apt to shut my mind to it, and although it was impossible

at that time, my loyalties were hopelessly divided. A Catholic who remembered that Sean O'Casey had served in the Irish Republican Army when its cause was truly respected, who had been in prison with Sean McStiofan and known and described him in *The Verdict of You All* as a passionate idealist who had been sentenced to eight years' imprisonment. 'If ever there was a case of men punished for the motive of their crime rather than the crime itself, this was it, for had the arms been stolen by boys from another school, the culprits would have been bound over.' As a non-party sympathizer with the weaker side in most struggles, I was yet an ex-soldier who knew that the British troops sent to Northern Ireland were the men, or the sons of the men, with whom I had served and sympathized with their cause. None of this brought me into the slightest conflict with my friends in Dun Laoghaire who like most true Irish in the South watched anxiously, were blind with fury at the accounts they heard of the so-called 'Bloody Sunday' and were exultantly present at the burning of the British Embassy in Dublin, though they made no boast of this to me. The situation in Belfast worsened during my time in Ireland and it was no longer possible to dismiss men like Paisley and Craig as exhibitionistic buffoons or to suppose that the fire of the IRA would burn itself out. But the nearer I was to that tragedy, the easier it was to be detached and never once, in my year in the country, was I made to feel uneasy or even embarrassed by the fact that I could not be wholly identified with any cause.

This consideration for the susceptibilities of an Englishman was not only shown by my young friends in Dun Laoghaire but by every Irishman I knew or had come to know since I had arrived. No one, except a particularly bloody-minded American whom I met in a Dublin pub, seemed to want to make me feel out-of-place as an Englishman in Ireland in these troubled times.

Certainly not Michael Killanin, a very old friend, who was that year to become President of the Olympic Games committee. I went to several parties at his Georgian house and met one of those remarkable miscellanies of people for which Dublin is renowned but no one of any particular interest to me except Michael himself.

Nor was I so isolated at Dun Laoghaire as might be supposed from this narrative. Friends from over the water came to stay with me, John Hitchcock of course, Ernst Thoma from Cologne, Steve Takaruk from Tangier, that other Steve who in an earlier chapter of this (on Gibraltar) was introduced as a humorously irresponsible ex-matelot. He was on his rather circuitous way from South Africa to Canada to try his luck on one of those semi-illicit enterprises which men of his kind follow adventurously till they outgrow such juvenilities.

There were also acquaintances from Dublin itself who came to discuss literary or other projects, Ulick O'Connor who had written a biography of Brendan Behan, and Christy Hudson a young postman who had written a play which I saw on its first night in a Lecture-room at the University converted to a small theatre, reminding me that the Irish who have written most of the best plays produced in England for the last century know how to enable their young playwrights to start their careers.

I remembered too that I had a godson, John Hitchcock's son Richard. He was, John told me, an avid collector of my books and professor of Spanish at Exeter University. He came across for a week-end and thereafter undertook to store in his home all the spare copies of my books and MSS which I have accumulated. This was a considerable boon to me who was already deciding that whatever I should do in the future I could not afford to cart all that printed and written matter about the world with me, though I did not wish to destroy it.

Richard was in his early thirties and I had not seen him for more than twenty years so that we were virtually strangers. He had all the eccentricities of a bibliophile and is a recognized authority—world authority is the term usually employed—on Muslim Spain. Since his father had been my closest friend for years before Richard was born I felt justified in sharing a little pride in his achievements, and I certainly do.

Another visitor to our big misshapen flat was the parish priest of Dun Laoghaire, a charming intellectual, the brother of a playwright and ex-Lord Mayor of Dublin. When I moved into the house I recovered a small sum in a libel dispute which I had made payable to him for parochial needs since I did not feel justified in accepting it myself, and he had repaid this by introducing to me a Compassionist Father, Edmund Burke, to whom Father Cuthbert Dunne who had baptized Oscar Wilde on his death-bed had bequeathed all his papers. This was too late to make any changes in my book, indeed none were strictly necessary, but enabled me later to nail for good certain other of Frank Harris's lies.

Glenageary House adjoined the great parish church built within the last fifty years to accommodate its enormous congregations. Nowhere, not even in Spain, have I seen so many thousands collecting by car, bus, motor-cycle and bicycle or on foot to any religious building for each of the six Sunday Masses said respectively in Latin (by the parish priest), in English, or in Irish. When I went with Joseph to Midnight Mass at Christmas every place in the stalls and aisles and on the outside steps was filled. The Irish I realized were not only a devout race but people with a strong, somewhat anachronistic, sense of convention.

To the surprise of both of us Joseph and I spent whole days in the summer of 1972 watching on television the Olympic Games, though neither of us had ever followed in newspaper or radio the events of any particular sport. They seemed to me, that year as ever (despite the racialist murders), one of the few achievements of our times which compare in civilization and beauty with the Olympic Games of the Ancient World from which they are unashamedly derived, and I would like to hear recordings of the conversation of modern athletes to compare with the words exchanged by the naked Greeks before their races. I do not believe they would greatly vary.

9

In May 1972 *The Unrecorded Life of Oscar Wilde* was published. In writing it I had exposed so many of the cherished myths about poor Oscar, tracing down and destroying the fatuous stories which were owed in origin to Frank Harris, Sherard and others that I did not expect it to be kindly received or a popular book and it was not. The best that Cyril Connolly could say of it was that it was the most 'sensible' account of Wilde and it made other critics feel so uncomfortable that they preferred to evade the issue. I was pleased that the *Times Literary Supplement* did not print one of those opinionated notices written by members of the teaching staff of redbrick universities who have replaced the professional writers of thoughtful criticism as in the editorial days of Bruce Richmond and Alan Pryce-Jones, particularly as I had known that once respected weekly suppress evidence of the misstatements it had published.

Printed reviews, in fact, even in the *Sunday Times* and *Observer*, have ceased to have much influence on the success or failure of books. Newspaper space is so limited that they can notice few new books, chiefly translations from East-European languages or would-be *avant garde* novels. I cannot pretend that as a professional writer I am worried about this for the sales of my books seemed to have been almost in inverse proportion to the space allotted to them in newspaper columns and I do not forget the supposed dictum of Joseph Conrad—'I do not read reviews of my books. I measure them'.

There have been writers in this century who have died heartbroken and embittered by the general neglect of their work after it had once received loud acclaim, and literary gossip in London names a number of them still living. This seems to me a foolish form of self-pity. Surely they must realize that novelty is all, as any maker of television commercials knows, promising *new* forms of every product he sells. It is natural enough that a writer with a new name, a new twist to his story, above all what is called a new angle, will make an appeal to those who have to fill newspaper space with material of the widest interest, and will make a headline out of that 'newness' before they consider the work, however admirable and however truly original, of a writer already well-known to their public. If they, the embittered writers, are honest they will admit that they themselves benefited by this altogether human state of things when they began to be published.

So I was not greatly concerned about the paucity of thoughtful reviews of *The Unrecorded Life of Oscar Wilde*, the most understanding of which came from Malcolm

Muggeridge, not in an English publication but in the American *Esquire*. I could perhaps afford this indifference because it chanced that BBC Television was running a series of films based on the fiction or life-story of Oscar Wilde and wanted me to appear on *Late Night Line Up*.

By now a dedicated viewer of television which provided the only form of entertainment practical on winter nights in Ireland, I had only once appeared on it in a guessing programme in the very early days and anticipated with considerable curiosity this occasion, which meant flying to London and staying the night. I did not find it in any way daunting though I shared the occasion, backed by a huge hoarding made from the dust-wrapper of my book, with Vyvyan Holland's widow who seemed rather bewildered since she, of course, had never known her father-in-law or much about him, Vyvyan himself, Wilde's son, having publicly confessed the paucity of his own recollections of his father. However, Sheridan Morley (whose father had played Wilde in one of the two films made about him) handled it all with the aplomb expected of a professional television interviewer—a new profession, by the way—and it all went off quite smoothly.

One result of it surprised me. I expected sales of the book to rise and they did so, but I did not expect that *Late Night Line Up* which I had thought to be an obscure afterthought of a programme would have such instant effect. Nothing had appeared in any published details of the item yet it seemed that everyone in England I had known since childhood chanced to be looking in that night and felt impelled to write and tell me so. I received dozens of letters and phone calls from friends I never thought would remember me, including one from a well-established Indian doctor I had last known as a medical student. From that point of view alone it was worth the visit to London but I also gained satisfaction in finding that I could appear on the box without seeming a novice.

10

I was pleased that the book, though no kind of best-seller, did comparatively well, but I was still anxiously concerned about money. I had sold the copyright of *The Unrecorded Life of Oscar Wilde* outright in both Great Britain and America and perhaps because I had refused to present the story in a wholly scandalous light—as I might have done on the strength of my friendship with Lord Alfred Douglas—I had little hope of it producing very much more financial benefit to me. Life in Ireland was expensive—far more so, as I have since discovered than in England—and I became somewhat alarmed by prospects of the future. At this point I read in *The Times* that a watercolour by Michael (Angelo) Rooker had been sold by Christie's for several thousand pounds and as I possessed another by this artist I wrote to Christie's and received a reply from one of their directors, Noël Annesley whom I knew to be an authority on Early English watercolours. He was coming to Ireland to visit his parents and would call and see me and look at the Rooker.

I started possessing early English watercolours in my twenties and had a quite considerable collection. It seemed to me that though I should miss this picture, of which I was proud, having bought it in open auction for £3 in Cheltenham in 1934, it would provide a solution to coming difficulties. Noël Annesley arrived and authenticated the drawing, but warned me that its condition—it had travelled with me and faced the strong sunlight of North Africa—would preclude it from fetching such a price as the one already sold by Christie's.

Now it happened that I had just received the munificent present of a painting from the artist responsible for it. The only modern painting I had ever bought was by Clifford Hall—a greatly admired portrait of the ballet dancer Leo Kersley in practice dress. This had gone under the hammer during the crisis I had suffered in 1953. Clifford had been sympathetic at the time and now wrote to me saying that he had found another portrait of Leo Kersley painted at the same time and would like me to have it to help me to forget that old injustice—almost unbelievable generosity from an artist. Of course I accepted it and have kept it ever since so that it hangs beside me as I write, made even more precious to me by the fact that a month or so ago, on Christmas Day 1973, at the height of an ever more successful career, Clifford had a heart attack and died.

But the point of this story here is that his gift arrived just as I had to decide about the Rooker and I could say yes to its sale. It was taken to London as I have recounted by the father of one of the boys, Ken Maher. When it came up for auction on June 6 1972 it fetched a thousand guineas.

This gave me a new idea. Since the Rooker had gone so satisfactorily why not the pottery I had collected so fondly? Why not *everything*? To cart about the world a houseful of furniture including several thousand books had been an intolerable burden and without all this impedimenta, and with the money it would produce, I could afford to live anywhere I liked for a year or two. Did I really want, I asked myself further, to remain on the outskirts of this ugly grey suburb of Dublin and face another sunless year in a country the beauty of whose landscapes was marred by lack of colour, where one waited weeks for the sun to light up the land and make it habitable to those not of totally hyperborean habit? Dublin had charm, beauty, grace and generosity; the countryside a loveliness surpassing most of Europe and the people had welcomed me, a foreigner of a race they regarded as enemies to all except the privileged and powerful, as a friend, but could I stand another winter of dripping trees around the house and in its rooms fires built by Joseph from expensive coal?

Once my mind had been entered by the tempting idea of owning nothing, using *être* rather than *avoir* as a staple verb, going back to the sun was all too easy. Professionally packed consignments of watercolours, glass, silver, 'oriental works of art' (I quote the catalogues which afterwards contained them), ceramics, porcelain, objects of vertu and antiquities were dispatched to Christie's while heavier furniture was sent to an auctioneer in Dublin and the flat was let to a family who took over at valuation the curtains and bookshelves and the rest which I had installed. Of my books I kept only a skeleton reference library and these with a few carpets and souvenirs of travel, blankets, sheets and clothes were packed and stored ready to be sent wherever I should decide to stay, (*not* to settle, I emphasized), and I prepared to leave the country.

In that orgy of non-possession I enjoyed myself not as Freudians would suggest with masochistic gusto, but because I honestly did not wish to 'set up house' in any permanent sense ever again.

My young Irish friends, the entire eleven of them with half a dozen of their current girl friends gave to Joseph and me a royal and rafter-raising farewell in the bar of the Elphin and rose before daybreak to see us off from the airport. I must, I suppose, describe my feelings with a cliché—

they were mixed, desperately mixed as the plane rose, not only from the airport but from an area of the past which would remain unforgettable to me. So *that* episode was finished.

Seven

Ceuta and Melilla

I would like to pretend that it was only when I reached the airport that I decided where I was going—it would not be true, but it was not entirely divorced from the truth. I had some idea of returning to North Africa—not Tangier or Tunis; somewhere between or near them, perhaps—but all I had decided after discussion with Joseph was to start by going to Paris where I could seek the advice of my boyhood's friend Robert Cahiza. I had warned him of my arrival with Joseph and he met us at the airport.

We spent a week in Paris including some time at Robert's country home, a huge converted farm-house which had in common with my one-time home Cage House a magnificent walnut tree and open lawns running down to high walls, covered with espalier'd fruit trees. One of the many directorships Robert held was in the South of Morocco and he suggested that we might try Ceuta, the Spanish port on Morocco's Mediterranean coast, so that he could call on us on his way southward. He had never been to Ceuta and knew only that it was a Spanish Free Port entirely surrounded by Moroccan territory but it might, he thought, be worth a try. I had visited it once in my early days in Tangier and knew that large quantities of liquor were smuggled from it into Morocco.

Still with an open mind we flew on to Madrid to stay with Cameron Rougvie, another old friend frequently referred to in these books. He is a Canadian and had left Tangier much as I had in the time of its increasing inhabitability. He gave one of his lavish dinner-parties for us and it was during this that I finally made up my mind. Another guest, a representative of some large concern—petroleum, I think—who knew Spain and North Africa spoke emphatically, and for no reason which he was able to give, forbiddingly against Ceuta. This aroused all my contrariness.

'You won't like it,' he promised me. 'Ghastly place.'

'In what way?'

'In every way. You'll hate it.'

'But why? Has it such a poor climate?'

He was bound to admit that the climate was pleasant.

'Is it expensive?'

No. It was a free port, he said. Cigarettes and whisky half the price that they were in Spain.

Was the town ugly? Dull? Tourist-ridden?

Well no. The buildings were like those of most Spanish towns with some fine old churches and open plazas. It was not dull because it was cosmopolitan and permissive. There were tourists in the summer but most of them came only on day trips from the Costa del Sol across the Straits. Then what *was* wrong? I persisted.

I must see for myself, he said. He was sure I should hate it. So obstinately I booked on the night train to Algeçiras and after a very choppy crossing arrived in Ceuta on an October afternoon of autumnal but still warm sunlight.

I remember that evening. I left the hotel to walk along the wide promenade by the sea and looked down on the movement below, hearing the fishermen calling from boat to boat. The promenade was brightly lit and crowded with Spanish conscripts and their girls, and the atmosphere was that mixture of Spanish and African which I remembered from my first days in Morocco. It was good to be back, I thought, good to have come South, to find the night air warm and the people aimless and contented. I was sure I had chosen well and confident that nothing could go wrong. I saw the shop windows on the landward side of the promenade piled with English and American goods, passed the Plaza de Africa with its benches under the palm-trees and its fifteenth-century cathedral. I believed that the Exchange Rate made living cheap for the English and that there was a British Consul in the city. I was, as I have been since boyhood, at home among Spaniards whose language I speak and write and I felt on that first evening, that I should be welcomed and happy in this place.

Next day I went to see the Consul, a Gibraltarian friend of Darrell Bates who had been established here since before the Spanish Civil War and during the difficulties over the Gibraltar issue. He told me of a building in the Plaza de Africa which had been divided into flats sometimes let to English visitors and warned me that it represented probably my only chance to find a furnished flat in the whole city. I soon realized that he was right and rented a flat on the second floor.

It was not long before the optimism of those first days began to erode and disillusionment to set in. The first hideous fact I realized about Ceuta was that there was *no fresh water* in the whole enclave and very little sea-water which had been put through a desalination process. None of the glamorous tourist booklets, full of coloured photographs, mentioned this basic fact and only someone who has lived under these conditions realizes how unpleasant they are. *All* water was cut off at some unfixed hour of the morning or early afternoon and although, of course, we filled the bath while it was still running this meant that we could never use it later in the day and the converted water gave off a peculiar odour.

Intolerable as this seemed it was only one aspect of a larger political imbroglio, the determination of Morocco to gain possession of Ceuta which had been occupied by Spain in 1580 and was definitely assigned to the Spanish crown by the Treaty of Lisbon in 1688. The Moors made several attempts to regain it and one siege under Mulai Islail lasted for twenty-six years. Since the gaining of independence by Morocco Ceuta has remained a thorn in Hispano-Moroccan relations and one of the arguments most frequently used against Spain by those who resist her claim to Gibraltar.

When I had first arrived in Tangier water in the town had been rationed. The shortage was caused because the Spanish, then in possession of all Northern Morocco, secured supplies to Ceuta, Villa San Jorge (as they called Alhucemas), and Tetuan, at the expense of Tangier which was international. When Morocco gained its freedom the position was reversed and Tangier had plentiful water supply while in Ceuta great plants had to be built to make sea-water potable. It was from these facts that I was suffering now. In hotels, restaurants and Government buildings the pressure continued for twenty-four hours so that visitors had no reason to know of the shortage but in the furnished flat I had taken I never knew when the supply would be cut off.

As time went on the inconvenience from this and other

G

causes increased. Rain clouds seemed to be trapped between the hills and the smiling streets I had seen at first grew slushy and torrents fell on the Plaza over which our windows looked. I found that I was still suffering enough from circulatory trouble to make the steep narrow staircase to the second floor difficult to negotiate. The posts and bank service were unreliable and much delayed while the cinemas in the town were unheated and showed nothing but Spanish films. But for two young teachers, English and French, who shared a flat on the top floor of our building we knew no one living in the town but Spaniards, a few Moroccans, Indians and Safarti Jews nearly all natives of Ceuta so that the notion of cosmopolitanism with which we had started proved to be totally false.

Still trying to reproduce some small semblance to life as it had been in Tangier some years before, we found a Fatima to do the housework but she begged a loan from Joseph on the plea of a sick baby and disappeared. A second spoke nothing but Arabic and was so old that she found the stairs more difficult than I did.

Moreover I came to realize that this free port which had grown up in years of corrupt trade and barter, of contraband and covetousness, had produced a population of people who, whatever their race, proved themselves to be greedy, usurious and unsociable. The Spanish, who all my life have seemed to me the best-mannered people in Europe, fought and shouted and argued over purchases in the market and even the Indian shopkeepers were sullen and discourteous, set on overcharging tourists.

There were only two restaurants of any repute in the town, one was in the Muralla, the principal hotel, where the service and food were showy but poor, the other was packed to the last place at lunchtime by 'groups' of package tourists with whom it had a contract, while at night the food consisted too obviously of reheated lunchtime dishes.

I had sent four suitcases from Dublin to Ceuta in order that they should arrive ahead of us but the expeditor, being more than usually Irish and dream-headed and finding that there was no airport in the Spanish enclave of Ceuta sent them to the neighbouring country of Morocco. It was only by chance that I heard they were lying unclaimed in Tangier airport and began devious efforts to recover them, making two journeys by hired car across the frontier and finally at some considerable expense obtaining them by employing one of those agents with wide acquaintance and knowledge of where to bestow largesse who are found in North Africa in crises of this sort. This did nothing to reconcile me to life in Ceuta which seemed full of such vexations.

The shops, which had looked so plentiful and promising at first, turned out, as usual in free ports, to sell goods needed by smugglers who hoped to get them over the frontier to Morocco, or past the Customs into England. There was little of use to an ordinary household in the town except at prices which tourists thought tempting till they reached their own frontiers, or realised that they were on the shelves of any English supermarket at lower prices. Whisky and cigarettes were marginally less expensive but one could not buy everyday goods like anchovy sauce, for instance, or condiments for making curry, or properly refined sugar or salt, or dried fruit anywhere in the town.

Moreover the value of the pound sterling against the peseta soon began to sink while English newspapers were unobtainable except by subscription and then arrived several days late. Perhaps most unpleasant of all was the arrogant and hostile attitude adopted towards the Moors by the colonial Spaniards, a relic of the time when the northern part of Morocco belonged to Spain and served largely as a recruiting ground. It was small wonder that the Moroccans were making their frontier with the enclave all but impassable and preventing Ceuta taxi-drivers from carrying fares to Tetuan as they had long been used to do. All this produced a disturbing sense of strain and impermanence. It seemed only a question of time before Ceuta would become, as Tangier had, a wholly Moroccan town with only the most uncomfortable affiliation with Europe.

2

But I had chosen Ceuta as a home and for a long time persisted in trying to create a *modus vivendi* there.

The area of the port, the Plaza de Africa in which we lived among the principal shopping streets was flanked on each side by hills, one of them rising steeply to a fortress called the Fortaleza de Monte Hacho, its slopes dotted with villas; the other hill of gentle inclines on which the old town of Ceuta was built. This was now a populous area named Hadu where cheap shops, cafés, eating-houses and decaying dwellings had narrow unpaved streets and poor lighting. It was evidently the brothel quarter of the garrison city and conscripts who had to return to barracks by ten o'clock every evening made the most of their time in the squalid places of entertainment. Few visitors to Ceuta knew or cared to know Hadu, but my curiosity was roused and I used to take a taxi to it and wander about on my own. There were some very curious things to be seen. Franco had said that the Spanish authorities do not need to concern themselves with homosexuality because in Spain it does not exist. He should have visited the bars of that quarter, ruled by some old half-caste hag who controlled the *maricones* she employed to amuse the *mili*—some no more than boys, some croaking old transvestites made up as prostitutes. The drink they sold was adulterated and noxious and the glasses unwashed. These bars could scarcely be called clip-joints, for Spanish soldiers do not usually have enough money to be 'clipped' but everyone in them was occupied in eliciting a drink from other customers or even a cigarette—unable to contain the predatory instincts of whores even when they themselves were seeking entertainment. I can see now some of the grotesquely painted faces of the unhappy queens who wore bits of tatty female dress and cheap jewelry and smelt of cheap scent and inferior brandy, aping not merely women but the lowest women, camp-followers at their most pitiful.

Even farther away from the centre of Ceuta was a shanty-town entirely populated by resentful Moors where, in mint-tea-bars I occasionally saw European beach-combers, deserters perhaps from the army of long ago, victims of *kif* or hashish. No area of the old International Zone of Tangier when it existed showed such poverty and squalor.

When I came to know some of the Spanish conscripts they invited me to a restaurant in Hadu where in a glass-covered patio behind shops in the main street only one dish was served but it was so good that the road outside was lined on Sunday mornings with the cars of the more prosperous citizens of Ceuta. The dish was roast chicken, unstuffed but impregnated with the scents and tastes of herbs very artfully cooked. They also took me to a more conventional café-restaurant on the seafront near my flat which had a cosmopolitan air to it where I spent many lazy evenings. One of them had been a men's hairdresser in civil life and as usual in the conscript army of Spain his talents were employed by the officers for most of his time in the service. He offered to cut my hair in return for the drinks I had invited him to.

'If I have to cut our Colonel's hair for nothing,' he said bitterly, 'I don't see why I shouldn't do it for a friend.'

He did so, most skilfully. Other conscripts through their similar useful abilities as motor mechanics, carpenters, painters and electricians, had earned the privilege of having passes that enabled them to wear civvies, all for the benefit of their officers who were, of course, regulars.

Christmas came and we made a pretence of celebrating it with the two schoolmasters who lived in our building, by ordering a festive lunch in the restaurant of the Muralla hotel, but it turned out to be anything but festive perhaps because Christmas Day is not much noticed in Spain—New Year's Eve being the great *fiesta*.

We made other efforts, joining a cinema club which was supposed to show films banned by the severe censorship of Spain. The club met in a chilly cinema and during our time in the town showed only one pre-war American comedy spoken with the original dialogue. We tried to enjoy cooking as we had wherever we had been but the calor gas stove was too small and rusty and the taste and shortage of water made it all pretty impossible.

Our best days were those on which we had visits from Tangier. One talkative widow who thought of moving to Ceuta came on several occasions till we were able to dissuade her from this foolhardy course, while Anna McKew and the Wiltons climbed our precipitous staircase to call on us sometimes. But as January passed we realized that though Ceuta was all right in theory and that in tourist leaflets it looked like a little paradise, it was not, to put it mildly, for us. It was pleasant to know that Our Lady of Africa to whom the old church in the Plaza was dedicated was not only the Patron Saint but the Officer Commanding the Ceuta garrison. It was amusing to drive to the peaks of the two hills and look back over the city which from those points looked white and inviting, but when one had descended and found the grey beaches of gritty schist and the uninviting market with its insolent stall-holders and the rapacious shopkeepers of the town, one became less interested in the fact that according to the brochures Ceuta shares with Rome, Carthage, Paris and others the characteristic of being built on seven hills. In fact, in spite of all these promised splendours and of the expense of having got myself and my few remaining possessions into the place I began to look for a way to escape.

3

There was only one remaining possibility so far as I could see. A night's journey by coastal steamer farther East from Ceuta was the Spanish city of Melilla, the other enclave which had remained in Spanish possession after the Independence of Morocco. I had visited it once by land and remembered that it was spacious and cheerful, with sandy beaches and open parks running up to the huge circle of buildings which made the centre of the town. Moreover the Moorish population, coming from nearer the Algerian frontier, were more lively and independent than those of Ceuta and there were far less tourists. I had very little hope of Melilla being what I had set out to find, a place in which to settle, but before I gave up all hope of this in North Africa I resolved to try once more.

We left Ceuta by a little coaster of the Compañia Transmediterranea at half an hour before midnight on Monday,

January 15 1973, knowing that the bumpy little ship would call at the Moroccan ports of Peñon Velez and Alhucemas where enough Spanish interests had remained after most Spaniards had left the country. I had visited both of these from the land but from the sea I could not recognize them. After the sun had risen and we had drunk strong ship's coffee the journey became a pleasant one, made in sparkling sunshine with much coming and going of highly miscellaneous passengers. We reached Melilla at five o'clock on the Tuesday afternoon and found to my disappointment that the big old nineteenth-century hotel, with tall over-furnished rooms, had been closed, nominally for repairs but in fact almost certainly for demolition, having been the subject of one of those interminable lawsuits which plague the commerce of Spain. Beside its site a new, boastfully modern Residencia Rusadir had been built, smartly furnished and adequately staffed, where rooms had been booked for us. But there was no catering—even breakfast having to be brought from the Bar-Restaurant Metropol which was five hundred yards away in the Circle, so that coffee arrived tepid and we were forced to lunch and dine in the town every day at considerable expense.

This meant that if we were to stay here at all, for a longer or shorter period, we must find a flat at once and on enquiry were told of a *corredor*, the Spanish equivalent of a house agent. His name was Cohen and he was a vigorous, honest man who set to work at once to find something suitable, reporting almost nightly to me in the little entrance lounge of the Rusadir. At first I had hopes of this for Cohen was of a sanguine nature and believed that there must be some premises to let, furnished or unfurnished, though he warned me that most houses and flats in Melilla changed hands only through sale and purchase. He took us to see a lower ground floor in which the ceiling was scarcely more than six feet high and the whole place more damp and cellar-like than that rejected in Dun Laoghaire nearly two years earlier. Undaunted by my refusal he found a third floor flat to which—I decided after the staircase at Ceuta—I could not climb. He raised our hopes many times and always refused any fee until he had found us a suitable home, while we remained at the *Residencia* knowing no one, receiving only rare communications from the outside world, all through the rest of January and February.

I liked Melilla. As a holiday resort it was almost unknown to the organisers of package tours and its fine open streets and gardens contrasted with the ill-paved alleys of Ceuta. There was good food to be had in the restaurants; shellfish and particularly giant prawns were plentiful, and most of the regional dishes of Spain could be found. Or, as the brochures claimed, with not too much exaggeration: 'Variety is perhaps the main feature of Melilla cookery. As the population is descended from people born in all parts of Spain, it is natural enough that the typical dishes of each province should be represented. Thus in Melilla one can enjoy Galician patties (*empanadas*), Asturian pork and beans (*fabada*), the chickpea stew (*cocido*) of Madrid, Valencian *paella* (rice with seafood and chicken etc.), and the always delicious fried fish which is so popular in Andalusia, whose specialities of *boquerones* and *chanquetes* are also caught in these waters. Other noteworthy dishes are the celebrated *marmita* and the *pinchitos*, of Arab origin.'

There was not much to be seen in the way of architecture and although I made a visit to Nador, the nearest Moroccan city fifty miles away I found very little of interest there.

But as I say I liked Melilla and was sorry that Señor Cohen could find nothing for us. Retrospectively I realize it was as well—my gregarious instincts would have been stifled by the isolation and provincialism of the place—but I remember those months spent in a last effort to make a home in North Africa as quite a cheerful time.

4

When I finally decided to abandon the search it was with more finality than that with which I had given up the various attempts at home-finding described in this book, and came from a strong and reasoned resolution to spend no more time in looking for ways to live pleasantly. I determined no longer to be a victim of what had become almost an obsession with this fruitless pursuit of the perfect way of life, but instead to get down to the work which means more to me than any background, to settle wherever and however I could, provided that I could write uninterrupted and Joseph could have the simple pleasures of the café and cinema which meant so much to him. Futile to spend my whole life and all the money I had raised from the sale of my possessions at Christie's in considering this city or that, whether the climate was right and whether I could find a suitable flat. Prodigal and foolish to worry about ways and means of reaching new places recommended for homes, only to discover the inevitable disadvantages that every place must have.

I realized, too, that unconsciously I had been looking for something which no longer existed—the city of Tangier as I had first found it in 1954, vibrant, lustful, amusing and civilized. I had once and for all to train my conviction as I had already trained my reason to recognize that there was no such place on the whole surface of the earth, and that even the Tangier I pictured in recollection was a mirage seen across the torrid years since that time.

Though it was true that travel and my efforts to settle are giving me today the material of this book, I recognized then as I do now that these produced a pretty egotistical and self-indulgent way of passing the years and I had something better to do than continue it. My literary energy was unimpaired, however hard I might find it to climb steep staircases or run for more than a few yards, and I had books to plan and write and many ways in which to satisfy the senses and appetites before I finally lost interest in pleasure.

So enough of all this. I would leave North Africa for good and take whatever home was offered to me.

Even then I had to decide where to go. I could cross from Melilla by ferry to Malaga and from there to Madrid, but then where? Being the creature of memory that I am I searched not the possibilities of the future but the recollections of the past and I came up with what seemed a reasonable solution; the Rhineland, Cologne, the Eifel—regions which had given me some of the happiest hours of my young manhood. So with no more fuss or doubt or reflexion I went by the midnight train from Malaga to Madrid, to stay with the Rougvies and tell them my plan, then took a plane to Frankfurt where I should be met by my friend of forty years' standing, Ernst Thoma.

Eight

Cologne

I can see with hindsight that to have gone back to Cologne
and the Eifel was to make too great a demand on the supposed benevolence and beauty of Germany and its people. I
have recalled in a number of the books in this sequence how
I first came to them on foot, in the course of what in a sadly
dated phrase could be called a walking tour, with my friend
John Hitchcock, how I returned to them again and again
and was writing my second novel in a little German town
when I received a telegram to say that my first novel had
been accepted; how I came to know a German boy named
Ernst Thoma, who in the years that followed claimed to
regard the coming of Hitler and the Second World War as
no more than an interruption in our friendship, which was
resumed as soon as communications made that possible. I
have confessed that although I spent six years in the Army
in the war against Nazism I never believed that it had
corrupted the German people as a whole or my friends in

particular and how I continued to return to Cologne and the Rhineland after I went to live in Tangier.

Pictures of the countryside which I had found in the early 1930s remained clear in my mind, the pine forests, the little pubs where one could drink litres of beer and eat and sleep for half the money that such entertainment cost in England, the pink and yellow country-women, buxom and hospitable to a foreigner, the dark beams and cross-beams on the fronts of old houses, the friendliness of everyone in the towns from Aachen to Cologne, the undergraduates of Bonn University with their peaked caps and rowdy beer-drinking, the country churches with their sharp little spires and devout congregations, the great walks I made, one of them from Bingen on the Rhine right through the Eifel to Monschau on the Belgian frontier, the plenitude and peace and content of those days in which my first literary ambitions were being satisfied and all Germany seemed to me to smile.

I had been there on a number of occasions since then but always by car and without any attempt to find the differences that time had made to the country. When I decided after leaving Melilla to return to Cologne I should have realized that whatever I convinced myself it would be like, I still had half in my mind that pre-Hitlerian Rhineland of long ago—dangerous and foolhardy illusions. I told myself that there must have been changes but I was quite unrealistic about them.

On the other hand I had to go somewhere and Ernst, now a paterfamilias nearing sixty, was still my friend and Cologne could not, I thought, be any more expensive than North Africa. As to the climate—after my eighteen months in Ireland I was prepared for anything. I thought I remembered enough of the language to make myself understood and I trusted in Joseph's linguistic facility to pick it up. I reminded myself foolishly how happy I had been in that country once and heard from Ernst that it was not impossible to find an inexpensive flat. All in all it did not seem such a bad plan.

When it failed it did so not for any of the petty reasons which had driven me from other places in which I had tried to settle, nor was it disappointment over the non-fulfilment of hopes based on old experience. It was not merely inconvenience, or the weather conditions, or the high cost of living, or the lack of entertainment, but something far more profound and disturbing than any of these. I discovered, indeed I became convinced, that whatever I had felt in young manhood, I had now come to dislike and distrust these people almost as much (though more from intuition than supposed experience) as a crusty old soldier who had in two wars against them, suffered from the devastation they had caused and illogically held them responsible for all his misfortunes. I came to detest Germans, positively and persistently, their towns and way of life, their conceit, their arrogance in authority and their obsequiousness when they felt mastered in even the most trivial respects. I had never before found myself living in a country so distasteful to me or among people I could not respect. Some causes for this may become evident but most were primal and instinctive and were held against all logic, all previous belief and all the accumulated sentiments I had gathered. They had no connection with the anti-German propaganda of war-makers or nationalists—propaganda I had always ignored or derided. I simply came through my own experience and perceptions to be repelled by a people whom I had once respected and liked, putting myself in doing so at variance with everyone about me.

2

It was all right at first. Ernst met us at Cologne station and took us to the modest hotel overlooking the Rhine where he had—with great difficulty, he said—found two rooms for us. It was cold, but in February that was to be expected and for the first few weeks my only preoccupation was the cost of the hotel and of the food we ate in restaurants and the realization that when I had been here only two years ago a pound sterling bought ten or twelve marks while now it bought only eight and was falling daily.

A flat was found in the suburb of Braunsfeld in a street of grey middle-class houses but convenient enough and within walking distance of the road car which ran into the city five miles away. The flat was to let unfurnished to anyone who would purchase the carpets, curtains and odd furniture of a young couple who wanted to live with in-laws. It was not excessively expensive so long as the pound fell no farther and it could be occupied at once. It was on the first floor, a fact that had become important to me in these recent years and although it was over a pub and belonged to an arbitrary old woman who lived on the ground floor, I ignored forebodings and moved in. Ernst worked for one of the great department stores, the Kaufhalle, and as a member of the staff could buy the goods I needed for the flat at the Kaufhof, its fellow-store, at a somewhat reduced price. Even so, to become established in that uninteresting street in the undustrial part of the city, cost me more than all my recent months in North Africa.

But I was anxious to settle and the flat with its two rooms, kitchen and bathroom, seemed adequate to me and Joseph as a place in which to eat, sleep and work—about the only things we could afford to do. As sanguine as ever we settled down, walking to the supermarkets in Aachenerstrasse for supplies once or twice a week, taking exercise in the Stadtgarten, or going into the city for the cinema now and then. I worked and slept in one of the two rooms, Joseph slept and worked in the other and we ate in the fairly large kitchen.

When Easter came we went to High Mass in the Cathedral, a ceremony which should have been magnificent. But the general belittlement of all the great Rites of the Church had infected Germany as it had most of the Christian world since the present Pope's attempts to popularize our religion. In any case the movement of tourists who walked about the aisles taking photographs not only of the ceremony but of their own friends in attitudes of prayer cheapened the occasion.

I thought of that Midnight Mass to which I had come to this cathedral in 1938 with the two sons of a circus family with whom I was travelling, and remembered the packed rows of men in uniform and the silence of that huge congregation, the chanting and the singing of the choir, the reverence and the dedication. Although most of those in that massive congregation were at war with us within the year and we ourselves were defending ourselves against them, that occasion had been unsullied and glorious. Thirty years later the cathedral interior seemed tawdry and dull.

However, Ernst still ran a large Opel car and took us out to Dusseldorf to the British Consulate where the magic stamp of membership of the Common Market gave me the right to remain in Germany. The men and women there were friendly and had read books of mine and the Consulate seemed what it should be to an Englishman alone in a foreign country, a haven of reassurance.

Not so the British Council whose responsibilities to an

author coming to live in the area should surely have been more marked. I wrote to the director on April 28 1973

Dear Mr Macdonagh,

  I expect to be living here for at least a year and should be most grateful if I may come and see you to discuss several points. Perhaps you would suggest a time when I may call?

  I wonder if you know Tom Morray of your organization? He was in Tunis when I was there the year before last.

Yours sincerely,
Rupert Croft-Cooke.

After I had waited ten days for a reply I received a letter from some minor official in the office telling me that 'if it was important I should see Mr Macdonagh' I should telephone him. This, of course, I ignored and it made me wonder yet again what exactly are the functions and value to British tax-payers of this exotic organization.

As some compensation for the disappointments and annoyances which were already disturbing me in Cologne, I went out to Monschau, the name of which village will already be familiar (perhaps too familiar) to readers of these books. The miracle was that any place of such intense appeal and beauty should still exist. It was crowded with sightseers who walked about the streets crying *'Wie schön!'* to one another, rowdy with the metallic battle-cries of motor cycles, and camped up with street lighting and window-boxes, while scarcely a private house remained in the little town, every one having been converted to a café, a souvenir store or a picture-postcard shop, but the river to which I had listened as I lay awake forty years ago still babbled over the stones and the castle and watch tower still over-looked the cobbled streets. Although the once rural Eifel had become industrialized and over-built, Monschau seemed to be the only remnant of the Germany I had known and loved.

I could no longer count Ernst Thoma as part of this. Only such a credulous loyalist as I would have expected to find in a man of sixty many traces of the idealistic and generous-hearted boy who had been among the dearest of my friends when we were young together, but I had not supposed that comparative failure in his career and separation from his wife after a long and unhappy marriage would have brought out the crudity and suspiciousness of his peasant origins, but this is what had happened. Every allowance had to be made for him, I recognized. A one-time victim of Nazi propaganda as he now revealed, he had known service at the Russian front on which both his younger brothers were killed and had heard his mother regret that he, not her youngest and favourite son, should be the one who survived. He had suffered relegation to a lower post in the firm he had served for thirty years and been disappointed in his son and daughter, who took their mother's side in the family feud and he was mortified by his son's success and the fact that he, the son, in that world of jealously watched salary scales, earned more than his father. His relationship with me continued but largely as a business matter—the calculation of his percentage on my purchases from the Kaufhof and the assessment of the cost of petrol when he used his car for my benefit. I was sorry for him and understood the pathos of his calamities but sympathy is a poor substitute for affection and respect. Above all what corroded that old and once impregnable friendship was the fact that I found I had forgotten most of my German and so was dependent on his goodwill for every little matter of daily life. I could not understand people who telephoned me or came to the door with papers (for it is a fallacy that most Germans in Cologne speak English). I could not get a haircut or a pair of shoes repaired or deal with matters connected with the landlady, or put an advertisement in the paper or call a doctor or complain of some annoyance without his aid as an interpreter with knowledge of Cologne. On the whole and for a long time he was obliging on a quid pro quo basis, but it meant a strain for both him and me and perhaps most of all for Joseph who values independence both on his own and on my behalf. Moreover Ernst was much occupied with his second home in which an emaciated girl suffering from the unnatural voraciousness of some wasting disease was the mother of his ten-year-old child.

Spring came but did not cheer the streets in which I lived. I remember looking out on the back yards behind the house one morning and asking myself what the *hell* I was doing in this dreary suburb of a German industrial city in which I had no friends or entertainment, no conversation except with Joseph and not even the compensation which television had given us in Ireland, since, perhaps with a touch of pique, I had decided that my German was not sufficient to make programmes comprehensible. I could, in the most modest way, have chosen any part of Europe as a home—why had I come here where but for the Dom there was nothing admirable to see and the bleak expanses of dwelling houses and tenements were relieved only by well-trodden public parks?

3

Three of the cinemas showed only blue films, and what a waste of time they were! I dislike pornography, though I would fight for the right of pornographers to create it. I was particularly bored by German films designed to stimulate old gentlemen with enlarged prostates perhaps because these films so lamentably failed in their object. Unoriginal, repetitious and silly, they differed from one another only in title and sometimes background; their humour was smutty and flat and they left one longing for the uncomplicated action of a Western. But in fairness to the German and Scandinavian films which were advertized weekly I was not much more entertained by *Last Tango in Paris* which I saw in Cologne.

There were other diversions. In one of the principal shopping streets were a number of so-called Sex shops, where you could buy Japanese female dolls or a plastic penis if you fancied, a whip or some extraordinary articles made of rubber or leather the exact purposes of which I was unable to understand. There were a number of bars frequented exclusively by homosexuals who, when gathered in such places always seem unattractive and sad in spite of much shrill hilarity. There was moreover a Turkish bath for their exclusive use where paunchy middle-aged men clucked over a few younger ones like possessive hens. None of these places interested me and when I was informed by a pretentious Irish cockney who called on me representing a club or society miscalled Gay Something-or-Other, even my indefatigable curiosity failed and I became aggressively occupied with the work I was doing.

I needed to do so. I was realizing daily what falls in the value of the pound meant to us in a country where life was already too costly. Medical and dental treatment for Joseph and me was ruinously expensive since it was not until after April 1 1973 that treatment under British National Health could be obtained by our nationals in Germany. The price of everything was such that we would not stop for a cup of coffee in our suburb or the city knowing that we might be presented with a bill—as we were once—for fourteen marks, then about two pounds.

For me this kind of restrictive economy, imposed by the expense of everyday life, was infuriating. I do not mind being poor so long as it does not curtail my freedom. Ever since my young manhood when to travel and seek experience in poverty was fun, I have managed one way or another to do what I liked, though by the grace of God my tastes were never extravagant. I had never been restrained from following minor impulses, and it made me dislike the people about me, besotted with plenty but calculating and unimaginative at the same time. From my father I inherited a determination not to be acquisitive or even thrifty, but to obtain value for money in small and large things and it had become a habit. In Germany it was impossible and this gave me yet another reason for discontent.

Prosperity did not suit the Germans. They expanded to the point of explosion under it and imported thousands of workers from under-privileged countries not—they hastily assured one—as slave labour as in Hitler's time, but with very little distinction in practice. One often saw more Turks, Tunisians, Portuguese and Moroccans on the streets than Germans. These immigrants lived in huge slum communities six or eight to a room and their presence seemed not to preoccupy the Germans as the Asian and African influx does the English, but to increase their self-importance, as though this Hitlerian dream at least had belatedly come true.

The Germans remained, I became convinced during the six months I lived amongst them, the blond Aryans arrogant in their racialism. For the first time since he had come to Europe with me thirty years earlier, Joseph was conscious of this and, as I shall recount, he had good reason to be. Functionaries of every kind from police to shop assistants were insolent and overbearing and though the old sign *strengstens verboten* had been suppressed at the time when Germans were weeping crocodile tears after the war, the spirit of order and prohibition persisted. If anyone supposes today that Adolf Hitler failed to leave his mark, that he is buried and forgotten except by a few madmen who keep alive his name and precepts, they have not made much study of the Germans today, and film and television directors who make such a point of repeating that it was *the Nazis* we fought against speak only half the truth.

The astonishing fact that they of all European people have succeeded best in finding statesmen of extraordinary breadth and vision, seems only to accentuate the common mediocrity.

Motoring there had become a madness, an obsession only slightly less dangerous than their passion for war in the 1930's. To be without a car was to lack one of the human senses, sight or hearing, and the last degradation of an unsuccessful man was when he had to part with his last mechanical conveyance. All motoring was at competitive speed and drivers had to be regulated by police-supervised road-crossings to allow pedestrians to run like rabbits to the other side once every ten minutes or so; and devil take the hindmost. Even then on the pavement the less agile walkers took their lives in their hands since drivers were allowed to park on the footpath and cruise along it to regain the road. Ernst Thoma, while I was in Cologne, was in the process of selling the family house which he had purchased with a mortgage twenty years before but he would not have thought of parting with his car. The internal combustion engine dominates the whole country like a fetish.

There were other aspects of Cologne life which I disliked though I daresay some of them were no more offensive than in London. Mugging and violence existed because—the Germans said—there were so many foreigners about. I witnessed a couple of cases of this, neither of which involved aliens, but since I could not read the local newspapers except with great difficulty I am not in a position to judge from the many hair-raising stories I heard.

4

In order to relieve the depression in the months of early summer, I decided to celebrate my seventieth birthday in the village in which I had spent my twenty-seventh, Monschau. I went over and found that although the Alte Herrlichkeit, the little hotel in which I had stayed, still existed, Frau Carl, whom I had seen since the war, had died a vigorous great-grandmother the year before and the premises had become a restaurant leased to a catering contractor. But the food was still good and the traditional dishes of the place, trout from the local river and venison from the forest, could still be obtained.

It was, I suppose, a sentimental idea to persuade my friends to join me in Monschau on that day, but it was an irresistible one to me and when I found that a number of them were prepared to make the difficult journey and stay the week-end I was tremendously excited by the prospect. It would be the first time that the three great friends of my young manhood, English, French and German, whom I have often described and contrasted in books, would meet, and it would delight me to see them together and with other old friends and relatives.

I did not in any but the purely mathematical sense believe

that I was seventy years old, and knew that I should feel—as I always do—immature among all these married couples and grandparents, but since this birthday would undoubtedly be my seventieth I might just as well make a celebration of the date. It falls almost exactly on Midsummer Eve, June 20 to be exact, and throughout the first days of June I looked forward to it as eagerly as a child.

5

Then befell something which not only confirmed my distrust and dislike of the Germans of today and persuaded me that racialism and beastliness lie just below the skin of most of them, but also convinced me that Hitler is alive, if not physically at least as a spirit in their hearts. It was so nearly incredible to me that I have kept and can produce all the documents in proof of it.

Joseph had been told on enquiry at the German Embassy in Madrid that no visa was necessary for him to enter Germany, and had seen evidence of the million or more Arabs and Turks working here. His papers had been passed on entry and I as his employer had been given whatever passport stamps were necessary by the British Consulate, so that we both supposed that *alles* was in *ordnung*. Both of us had been required by the Health Department to produce medical certificates obtained at great trouble and expense but we had supposed that this was a piece of that form-filling and formality to be expected in this meticulous country of countless Government employees.

Now he suddenly received an official notice to attend at an office with a seventeen-letter composite name at a certain time. He found a sizable hallway in some public department for foreigners crowded from end to end with several hundred men, mostly Arabs and Turks, some of whom said they had been waiting for many days to apply for working permits.

After some hours of waiting in a noisome atmosphere Joseph was admitted to an office in which was a young man who looked like a guard in a television film depicting Colditz, and was told at once that he was in Germany illegally and must leave immediately. Joseph explained that he had been told by the German consulate in Madrid that he needed no document to enter and the young man said that this was so; 'to *enter*, but not to *stay*'. Joseph then explained that he was here on a private visit with me for whom he had worked as a secretary for thirty years, and showed his passport and mine to prove it. The young man's reply was to put a large stamp in Joseph's passport giving him notice to leave the country in seven days' time. If he wanted to remain he must go back to the country in which he had last been a resident (Ireland) and apply to the German Embassy there for a work permit. When Joseph pointed out the impracticability of such a course, keeping to himself any mention of the absurdity, the official closed the interview.

I had heard of such things for displaced persons, refugees, suspects of Interpol, victims of Amin, would-be foreign workers in a trade already overcrowded in England or other unfortunates who had fallen foul of regulations but I simply could not believe that in a civilized Western country it could happen without any reason whatever to a man who was not guilty of the smallest offence, who had sufficient means to maintain himself in the country and had a home in it. As we discovered later, the explanation lay in the fact that Joseph had a darker complexion than most of the Arab workers and was not necessary to German industry. These

were the old catchwords and distinctions of Hitler's time—
the only difference being that in the days of Nazi domination
non-Aryans were sent to the gas-chambers while today
officials were satisfied with peremptorily expelling Joseph
from the country without any pretence of reason. That, it
must be admitted, was a vital difference, but it was, after all,
only one of degree.

Since this happened less than a month before the day on
which my party in Monschau was planned, urgent steps had
to be taken and I at once consulted a firm of solicitors of high
repute, Messrs Theo and Gunter Oberle, and one of the
partners took the matter up immediately. He found the
official who had made the order but whose name was never
revealed (though he can, of course, be identified). This man
was pressed by the lawyer to say *why* he had done anything
so arbitrary and could give no reason at all. He believed it
was the 'usual proceeding' with Indian nationals. He refused
to rescind his order but after the lawyer had seen higher
officials, who were evidently alarmed at possible revelations
about the system or the man who had enforced it, I was
asked how long I wanted to remain in Germany with
Joseph. Suppressing the impulse to say not a minute longer,
I opted for a month, that was until my birthday party was
over, and Joseph was granted that time.

My party, then, would be a farewell to the country in
which I had once been happy. It would take place as I
planned and immediately after it I would leave for England.
The incident left me with a conviction that a Nazi is
wrapped in the skin of most Germans and even if that
conclusion is unfair and untrue, I want nothing more to do
with these people during what may remain of my life, and
when I read of Germans complaining of the popularity of
war films on British television I wonder at their impudence.

6

John Hitchcock and I had first walked into Monschau from Rötgen where we had crossed into Germany from Belgium on the previous day. I described this in *The Last of Spring* as a climax to most of my life that had gone before. 'The climax lay partly in the nature of the place but more in my response to it, for it was as though I had come on something that all my life I had been seeking. Monschau is beautiful—not a doubt of that. It is called, in fact, the Pearl of the Eifel. It is old, picturesque, full of atmosphere and the thousands of visitors who stare at it in summer respond kindly to its charm. '*Wie schön!*' and '*Wunderbar!*' they repeat audibly as they march through the narrow streets. But to none of them does it mean, I think, what it meant to me that summer noon when I first found it, a month after my twenty-sixth birthday.'

In those days the hotel we chose, the *Alte Herrlichkeit* was owned and administered by a family consisting of white-haired Herr Muller, a German of the old school who retained his loyalty to the Kaiser and wore a frock coat and top hat to attend Mass on Sundays, his daughter Frau Carl a bright buxom woman of forty and her leggy fifteen-year-old daughter Paula. During that year and the following I stayed for long periods in the hotel, where full board cost forty marks a week, and when I returned to Monschau twenty-five years later (in 1955) Herr Muller had died, Frau Carl still administered the hotel and Paula had a husband and two sons approaching twenty. Now, in 1973 Frau Carl had died in the previous year, Paula was a grandmother and the *Alte Herrlichkeit* had become a restaurant leased to a caterer from Cologne. But the tobacconist's shop in the town was still owned by Erich, the mischievous son of the proprietor of my day, and Paula had built herself a large private house in which she let a few hotel rooms on one of the steep hills overlooking the town. Many of the people in Monschau who remembered me as a boy were amused and pleased at my symbolic return to celebrate my seventieth birthday and welcomed a gesture so sentimental and in key with their own traditions. Paula let me what rooms she had available so that some of my guests would be accommodated on the hill while the others would stay in a seventeenth century house in the town. And Paula gave me the use of her own big sitting-room in which to collect my friends for a cocktail party before we went down to the *Alte Herrlichkeit* to dine.

The evening was, in a sense, the most significant and rewarding of my life. My formal hostess was Joan Cave who as young Joan Killick had teased and looked after my brother Laurie and me when we rented a thatched cottage at the end of their tea-gardens in Wrotham a year or two after I had discovered Monschau. She had a son whom she had, to my delight, sent to Tonbridge and whose whole life I had watched from crawling babyhood to his marriage and success as a doctor in recent years. He was bringing his pretty young wife to my party and the three of them, Joan, David and Anne Cave would come by car.

Patrick Kinross, a friend in a different manner, who had supported me in the crisis of 1953 and been my host at his London house in 'Little Venice' at intervals ever since, was the only fellow-writer who would be there. A year younger than me and pressed by work and engagements it would not be easy for him to come, by air to Aachen and by car from there and I loved him for making the effort. John Hitchcock and his wife Marjorie crossed on the night before and stayed in Aachen, while Robert Cahiza, another friend of forty years' standing who will be familiar to readers of this series of books, came up from Paris with Antoinette.

To introduce the only relative of mine who came it is necessary to return to the early fastnesses of this series of books where the curious may find recorded in *The Gardens of Camelot* that my father's great friend and fellow-blue-button when they were both clerks to Marnham and Company, a firm of stockbrokers, was a man named Edward Taylor. He introduced my father to his sister Lucy who became my father's wife and my mother. Edward Taylor himself married my Aunt Mary, a most lovable old lady who had been one of the only members of my family of whom I was fond. One of the daughters of Edward and Mary Taylor was my Cousin Audrey and she in turn married a naval officer named Oliver. Their son Stephen while at Oxford had made expeditions to the Atlas Mountains and brought numbers of his undergraduate friends to my home in Tangier. Now a barrister and married to a lovely girl named Dawn he would come by car to Monschau for my party and very glad and grateful for that I was.

Ernst Thoma would bring the mother of his youngest child, the poor girl who had the affliction of never being able to stop eating while remaining wasted in body, and there would also be Donald Ebrahim, the Indian doctor who had been my friend since his days as a medical student and of course the dearest and closest of all, my secretary and (in all but the legal sense) adopted son, Joseph. Sixteen people would sit down to dinner at a long table in the *Alte Herrlichkeit*, in surroundings familiar to me, as at least half of them had been, for the best part of forty years. If that was not sentimentalising, what is?

I had insisted on no black ties or speeches and I had

promised the traditional dishes of Monschau. The dinner would be simple but I could trust every item of it and when Robert Cahiza brought from Paris the beautifully printed menus which were his gift for the occasion, I felt I had chosen aptly.

Dîner
Truite de l'Eifel au Bleu
Pommes de terre á l'anglaise
Sauce au raifort
Beurre à la meunière

Selle de Chevreuil à l'Allemande
Croquettes de pommes de terre
Girolles
Compote d'airelle

Monschauer Dutchen

Vins
Oestricher Lenchen Riesling
Spätlese 1966

Walporzheimer Pfaffenberg
Spätburgunder Kabinett 1971

Thank God I had stipulated no speeches. I was driven up the hill and put to bed in my room in Paula's house, not drunk, but quite exhausted by the intense and wonderful happiness of the occasion, the last words I remember being Robert Cahiza's exhortation that the fête must be repeated every year hereafter in Paris.

The evening made a splendid epilogue not only to my stay in Germany (for which it was a final one) but for all my travelling in the years since I had left Tangier, or perhaps it may be, for all my travelling, period. I was going home with no doubt about the use of the word. Even the route, from Cologne by train to Ostend, across the Channel to Dover and up to London, was a familiar one, and my spirits rose to it.